GRANTA 73, SPRING 2001
www.granta.com

EDITOR *Ian Jack*
DEPUTY EDITORS *Liz Jobey, Sophie Harrison*
EDITORIAL ASSISTANT *Fatema Ahmed*

CONTRIBUTING EDITORS *Neil Belton, Pete de Bolla, Ursula Doyle,*
Will Hobson, Gail Lynch, Blake Morrison, Andrew O'Hagan, Lucretia Stewart

ASSOCIATE PUBLISHER *Sally Lewis*
FINANCE *Geoffrey Gordon*
SALES *Claire Gardiner*
PUBLICITY *Alex Hippisley-Cox*
SUBSCRIPTIONS *John Kirkby, Darryl Wilks, Chris Bennett*
PUBLISHING ASSISTANT *Mark Williams*
ADVERTISING MANAGER *Kate Rochester*

PUBLISHER *Rea S. Hederman*

Granta, 2-3 Hanover Yard, Noel Road, London N1 8BE
Tel 020 7704 9776 Fax 020 7704 0474
e-mail for editorial: editorial@granta.com

Granta US, 1755 Broadway, 5th Floor, New York, NY 10019-3780, USA

TO SUBSCRIBE call 020 7704 0470 or e-mail subs@granta.com
A one-year subscription (four issues) costs £24.95 (UK), £32.95 (rest of Europe) and £39.95 (rest
of the world).

Granta is printed in the United States of America. The paper used in this publication meets the
minimum requirements of American National Standard for Information Sciences—Permanence of
Paper for Printed Library Materials, ANSI Z39.48-1984. ∞

Granta is published by Granta Publications and distributed in the United States by Granta Direct
Sales, 1755 Broadway, 5th Floor, New York, NY 10019-3780, USA.
This selection copyright © 2001 Granta Publications.

Design: Random Design.
Front cover photograph: Raymond Depardon/Magnum; back cover photographs: Manuel
Bauer/Lookat; Hulton Getty

Extract from Eucalyptus by Murray Bail. First published in Great Britain by The Harvill Press in
1998. © Murray Bail, 1998. Reproduced by permission of The Harvill Press.

ISBN 0 903141 42 6

catfish & mandala

a vietnamese odyssey **andrew x. pham**

flamingo

GRANTA 73

Necessary Journeys

What happened when the hippy spirit of Ken Kesey's Merry Pranksters met the English innocence of Cliff Richard's Summer Holiday?

Take a ride back in time on *The Bus*.

In July 1973 21-year-old Daniel Meadows, fresh out of art school, bought a double-decker bus and set off round England in search of ordinary people to photograph. He took money from the Arts Council and from big business and for 14 months he offered free portrait sessions to the working people of 22 different towns.

A quarter of a century later Meadows came across these photographs in his archive and began to wonder what had happened to the people in the pictures. So he set out again in search of them.

Many could not be found, others had died, but a number of people turned up to be re-photographed. The result is a powerful pictorial history of the changing state of England, the vagaries of fashion, and the ravages of time.

Meadows also interviews the sitters, ordinary people from different walks of life, who talk candidly about their lives, their friends, their loves, their families and what they feel the future holds.

DANIEL MEADOWS

THE BUS

THE FREE PHOTOGRAPHIC OMNIBUS
1973–2001

Published in May as an illustrated paperback at £15.00
Available from all good bookshops
or order by telephone (01476 541 000)
or online from www.harvill.com
postage free within Europe

THE HARVILL PRESS

DUNKIRK
Ian McEwan

There were horrors enough, but it was the unexpected detail that threw him and afterwards would not let him go. When they reached the level crossing, after a five kilometre walk along a narrow road, he saw the path he was looking for meandering off to the right, then dipping and rising towards a copse that covered a low hill to the north-west. They stopped so that he could consult the map. But it wasn't where he thought it should be. It wasn't in his pocket, or tucked into his belt. Had he dropped it, or put it down at the last stop? He let his greatcoat fall on the ground and was reaching inside his jacket when he realized. The map was in his left hand and must have been there for over an hour. He glanced across at the other two but they were facing away from him, standing apart, smoking silently. It was still in his hand, and he had prised it from the dead hand of a captain in the West Kents lying in a ditch outside—outside where? The rear area maps were rare. He also took the captain's revolver. He wasn't trying to impersonate an officer. He had simply lost his rifle and intended to survive.

The path he was interested in started down the side of a bombed house, fairly new, perhaps a railwayman's cottage rebuilt after the last time. There were animal tracks in the mud surrounding a puddle in a tyre rut. Probably goats. Scattered around were shreds of striped cloth with blackened edges, remains of curtains or clothing, and a smashed-in window frame draped across a bush, and everywhere, the smell of damp soot. This was their path, their short cut. He folded the map away, and as he straightened from picking up the coat and was slinging it around his shoulders, he saw it. The others, sensing his movement, turned round, and followed his gaze. It was a leg in a tree. A mature plane tree, only just in leaf. The leg was twenty feet up, wedged in the first forking of the trunk, bare, severed cleanly above the knee. From where they stood there was no sign of blood or torn flesh. It was a perfect leg, pale, smooth, small enough to be a child's. The way it was angled in the fork, it seemed to be on display, for their benefit or enlightenment: this is a leg.

The two corporals made a dismissive sound of disgust and picked up their stuff. They refused to be drawn in. In the past few days they had seen enough.

Nettle, the lorry driver, took out another cigarette and said, 'So, which way, Guv'nor?'

11

They called him that to settle the difficult matter of rank. He set off down the path in a hurry, almost at a half run. He wanted to get ahead, out of sight, so that he could throw up, or crap, he didn't know which. Behind a barn, by a pile of broken slates, his body chose the first option for him. He was so thirsty, he couldn't afford to lose the fluid. He drank from his canteen, and walked around the barn. He made use of this moment alone to look at his wound. It was on his right side, just below his ribcage, about the size of a half-crown. It wasn't looking so bad after he washed away the dried blood yesterday. Though the skin around it was red, there wasn't much swelling. But there was something in there. He could feel it move when he walked. A piece of shrapnel perhaps.

By the time the corporals caught up, he had tucked his shirt back in and was pretending to study the map. In their company the map was his only privacy.

'What's the hurry?'

'He's seen some crumpet.'

'It's the map. He's having his fucking *doubts* again.'

'No doubts, gentlemen. This is our path.'

He took out a cigarette and Corporal Mace lit it for him. Then, to conceal the trembling in his hands, Robbie walked on, and they followed him, as they had followed him for two days now. Or was it three? He was lower in rank, but they followed and did everything he suggested, and to preserve their dignity, they teased him. When they tramped the roads or cut across the fields and he was silent for too long, Mace would say, 'Guv'nor, are you thinking about crumpet again?' And Nettle would chant, 'He fucking is, he fucking is.' They were townies who disliked the countryside and were lost in it. The compass points meant nothing to them. That part of basic training had passed them by. They had decided that to reach the coast, they needed him. It was difficult for them. He acted like an officer, but he didn't even have a single stripe. On the first night, when they were sheltering a while in the bike shed of a burnt-out school, Corporal Nettle said, 'What's a private soldier like you doing talking like a toff?'

He didn't owe them explanations. He intended to survive and he didn't care whether they tagged along or not. Both men had hung on to their rifles. That was something at least, and Mace was a big man, strong across the shoulders, and with hands that could have spanned two octaves of the pub piano he said he played. Nor did Robbie mind about the taunts. All he wanted now as they followed the path away from the road was to forget about the leg. Their path joined a track which ran between two stone walls and dropped down into a valley that had not been visible from the road. At the bottom was a brown stream which they crossed on stepping stones set deep in a carpet of what looked like miniature water parsley. Their route swung to the west as they rose out of the valley, still between the ancient walls. Ahead of them the sky was beginning to clear a little and glowed like a promise. Everywhere else was grey. As they approached the top through a copse of chestnut trees, the lowering sun dropped below the cloud cover and caught the scene, dazzling the three soldiers as they rose into it. How fine it might have been, to end a day's ramble in the French countryside, walking into the setting sun. Always a hopeful act.

As they came out of the copse they heard bombers, so they went back in and smoked while they waited under the trees. From where they were they could not see the planes, but the view was fine. These were hardly hills that spread so expansively before them. They were ripples in the landscape, faint echoes of vast upheavals elsewhere. Each successive ridge was paler than the one before. He saw a receding wash of grey and blue fading in a haze towards the setting sun, like something oriental on a dinner plate.

They were making a long traverse across a deeper slope that edged further to the north and delivered them at last to another valley, another little stream. This one had a more confident flow and they crossed it by a stone bridge thick with cow dung. The corporals, who were not as tired as he was, had a lark, pretending to be revolted. One of them threw a dried lump of dung at his back. Robbie did not turn round. The scraps of cloth, he was beginning to think, might have been a child's pyjamas. A boy's. The dive-bombers sometimes came over not long after dawn. He was trying to push it away, but it would not let him go. A French boy asleep in his bed. Robbie needed to put more distance between himself and that bombed cottage. It was not only the German army and air force pursuing him now. If there had been a moon he would have been happy walking all night. The corporals wouldn't like it. Perhaps it was time to shake them off.

Downstream of the bridge was a line of poplars whose tops fluttered brilliantly in the last of the light. They turned in the other direction and soon the track was a path again and was leaving the stream. They wound and squeezed their way through bushes with fat shiny leaves. There were also stunted oaks, barely in leaf. The vegetation underfoot smelled sweet and damp, and he thought there must be something wrong with the place to make it so different from anything they had seen.

Ahead of them was the hum of machinery. It grew louder, angrier, and suggested the high velocity spin of flywheels or electric turbines turning at impossible speed. They were entering a great hall of sound and power.

'Bees!' he called out. He had to turn and say it again before they heard him. The air was already darker. He knew the lore well enough. If one stuck in your hair and stung you, it sent out a chemical message as it died and all who received it were compelled to come and sting and die at the same place. General conscription! After all the danger, this was a kind of insult. They lifted their greatcoats over their heads and ran on through the swarm. Still among the bees, they reached a stinking ditch of slurry which they crossed by a wobbling plank. They came up behind a barn where it was suddenly peaceful. Beyond it was a farmyard. As soon as they were in it, dogs were barking and an old woman was running towards them flapping her hands at them, as though they were hens she could shoo away. The corporals depended on Robbie's French. He went forward and waited for her to reach him. There were stories of civilians selling bottles of water for ten francs, but he had never seen it. The French he had met were generous, or otherwise lost to their own miseries. The woman was frail and energetic. She had a gnarled, man-in-the-moon face and a wild look. Her voice was sharp.

'C'est impossible, M'sieu. Vous ne pouvez pas rester ici.'

'We'll be staying in the barn. We need water, wine, bread, cheese and anything else you can spare.'

'Impossible!'

He said to her softly, 'We've been fighting for France.'

'You can't stay here.'

'We'll be gone at dawn. The Germans are still...'

'It's not the Germans, M'sieu. It's my sons. They are animals. And they'll be back soon.'

Robbie pushed past the woman and went to the pump which was in the corner of the yard, near the kitchen. Nettle and Mace followed him. While he drank, a girl of about ten and an infant brother holding her hand watched him from the doorway. When he finished and had filled his canteen he smiled at them and they fled. The corporals were under the pump together, drinking simultaneously. The woman was suddenly behind him, clutching at his elbow. Before she could start again he said, 'Please bring us what I asked for or we'll come in and get it for ourselves.'

'My sons are brutes. They'll kill me.'

He would have preferred to say, So be it, but instead he walked away and called over his shoulder, 'I'll talk to them.'

'And then, M'sieu, they will kill you. They will tear you to shreds.'

Corporal Mace was a cook in the same RASC unit as Corporal Nettle. Before he joined he was a warehouseman at Heal's in the Tottenham Court Road. He said he knew a thing or two about comfort and in the barn he set about arranging their quarters. Robbie would have thrown himself down on the straw. Mace found a heap of sacks and with Nettle's help stuffed them to make up three mattresses. He made headboards out of hay bales which he lifted down with a single hand. He set up a door on brick piles for a table. He took out half a candle from his pocket. 'Might as well be comfy,' he kept saying under his breath. It was the first time they had moved much beyond sexual innuendo. The three men lay on their beds, smoking and waiting. Now they were no longer thirsty their thoughts were on the food they were about to get and they heard each other's stomachs rumbling and squirting in the gloom, and it made them laugh. Robbie told them about his conversation with the old woman and what she had said about her sons.

'Fifth columnists, they would be,' Nettle said. He only looked small alongside his friend, but he had a small man's sharp features. He had a friendly, rodent look, heightened by his way of resting the teeth of his upper jaw on his lower lip.

'Or French Nazis. German sympathizers. Like we got Mosley,' Mace said.

They were silent for a while, then Mace added, 'Or like they all are in the country, bonkers from marrying too close.'

'Whatever it is,' Robbie said, 'I think you should check your weapons now and have them handy.'

They did as they were told. Mace lit the candle, and they went through the routines. Robbie checked his pistol and put it within reach. When the corporals were finished, they propped the Lee-Enfields against a wooden crate and lay down on their beds again. Presently the girl came with a basket. She set it down by the barn door and ran away. Nettle fetched the basket and they spread out what they had on their table. A round loaf of brown bread, a small piece of soft cheese, an onion and a bottle of wine. The bread was hard to cut and tasted of mould. The cheese was good, but it was gone in seconds. They passed the bottle around and soon that was gone too. So they chewed on the musty bread and ate the onion.

Nettle said, 'I wouldn't give this to my fucking dog.'

'I'll go across,' Robbie said, 'and get something better.'

'We'll come too.'

But for a while they lay back on their beds in silence. No one felt like confronting the old lady just yet.

Then, at the sound of footsteps they turned and saw two men standing in the entrance. They each held something in their hands, a club perhaps, or a shotgun. In the fading light it was not possible to tell. Nor could they see the faces of the French brothers.

The voice was soft. *'Bonsoir, Messieurs.'*

'Bonsoir.'

As Robbie got up from his straw bed he took the revolver. The corporals reached for their rifles. 'Go easy,' he whispered.

'Anglais? Belges?'

'Anglais.'

'We have something for you.'

'What sort of thing?'

'What's he saying?' one of the corporals said.

'He says they've got something for us.'

'Fucking hell.'

The men came a couple of steps closer and raised what was in their hands. Shotguns surely. Robbie released his safety catch. He heard Mace and Nettle do the same. 'Easy,' he murmured.

'Put away your guns, *Messieurs*.'

'Put away yours.'

'Wait a little moment.'

The figure who spoke was reaching into his pocket. He brought out a torch and shone it not at the soldiers, but at his brother, at what was in his hand. A French loaf. And at what was in the other hand, a canvas bag. Then he showed them the two baguettes he himself was holding.

'And we have olives, cheese, pâté, tomatoes and ham. And naturally, wine. *Vive l'Angleterre*.'

'Er, *vive la France*.'

They sat at Mace's table which the Frenchmen, Henri and Jean-Marie Bonnet, politely admired, along with the mattresses. They were short, stocky men in their fifties. Henri wore glasses, which Nettle said looked odd on a farmer. Robbie did not translate. As well as wine, they brought glass tumblers. The five men raised them in toasts to the French and British armies, and to the crushing of Germany. The brothers watched the soldiers eat. Through Robbie, Mace said that he had never tasted, never even heard of, goose liver pâté, and from now on, he would eat nothing else. The Frenchmen smiled, but their manner was constrained and they seemed in no mood to get drunk. They said they had driven all the way to a hamlet near Arras in their flatbed farm truck to look for a young cousin and her children. A great battle had been fought for the town but they had no idea who was taking it, who was defending it or who had the upper hand. They drove on the back roads to avoid the chaos of refugees. They saw farmhouses burning, and then they came across a dozen or so dead English soldiers in the road. They had to get out and drag the men aside to avoid running over them. But a couple of the bodies were almost cut in half. It must have been a big machine gun attack, perhaps from the air, perhaps an ambush. Back in the lorry, Henri was sick in the cab, and Jean-Marie, who was at the wheel, got into a panic and drove into a ditch. They walked to a village, borrowed two horses from a farmer and pulled the Renault free. That took two hours. On the road again, they saw burnt-out tanks and armoured cars, German as well as British and French. But they saw no soldiers. The battle had moved on. By the time they reached the hamlet, it was late afternoon. The place had been completely destroyed and was deserted. Their cousin's house was smashed up, with bullet holes all over the walls, but it still had its roof. They went in every room and were relieved to find no one there. She must have taken the children and joined the thousands of people on the roads. Afraid of driving back at night, they parked in a wood and tried to sleep in the cab. All night long they heard the artillery pounding Arras. It seemed impossible that anyone, or anything, could survive there. They drove back by another route, a much greater distance, to avoid passing the dead soldiers. Now, Henri explained, he and his brother were very tired. When they shut their eyes, they saw those mutilated bodies.

Jean-Marie refilled the glasses. The account, with Robbie's running translation, had taken almost an hour. All the food was eaten. He thought about telling them of his own single, haunting detail. But he didn't want to add to the horror, and nor did he want to give life to the image while it remained at a distance, held there by wine and companionship. Instead, he told them how he was separated from his unit at the beginning of the retreat, during a Stuka attack. He didn't mention his injury. The Frenchmen might have shown concern, and he didn't want the corporals to know about it. Instead he explained how they were walking cross-country to Dunkirk to avoid the air raids along the main roads.

Jean-Marie said, 'So it's true what they're saying. You're leaving.'

'We'll be back.' He said this, but he didn't believe it.

The wine was taking hold of Corporal Nettle. He began a rambling eulogy of what he called 'Frog crumpet'—how plentiful, how available, how delicious. It was all fantasy. The brothers looked at Robbie.

'He says French women are the most beautiful in the world.'

They nodded solemnly and raised their glasses.

They were all silent for a while. Their evening was almost at an end. They listened to the night sounds they had grown used to—the rumble of artillery, stray shots in the distance, a booming far-off explosion—probably sappers blowing a bridge in the retreat.

'Ask them about their mum,' Corporal Mace suggested. 'Let's get that one cleared up.'

'We were three brothers,' Henri explained. 'The eldest, Paul, her firstborn, died near Verdun in 1915. A direct hit from a shell. There was nothing to bury apart from his helmet. Us two, we were lucky. We came through without a scratch. Since then, she always hated soldiers. But now she's eighty-three and losing her mind, it's an obsession with her. French, English, Belgian, German. She makes no distinction. You're all the same to her. We worry that when the Germans come, she'll go at them with a pitchfork and they'll shoot her.'

Wearily, the brothers got to their feet. The soldiers did the same.

Jean-Marie said, 'We would offer you hospitality at our kitchen table. But to do that, we would have to lock her in her room.'

'But this has been a magnificent feast,' Robbie said.

Nettle was whispering in Mace's ear and he was nodding. Nettle took from his bag two cartons of cigarettes. Of course, it was the right thing to do. The Frenchmen made a polite show of refusing, but Nettle came round the table and shoved the gifts into their arms. He wanted Robbie to translate.

'You should have seen it, when the order came through to destroy the stores. Twenty thousand cigarettes. We took whatever we wanted.'

A whole army fleeing to the coast, armed with cigarettes to keep the hunger away.

The Frenchmen gave courteous thanks, complimented Robbie on his French, then bent over the table to pack the empty bottles and glasses into the canvas bag. There was no pretending that they would meet again.

'We'll be gone at first light,' Robbie said. 'So we'll say goodbye.'

They shook hands.

Henri Bonnet said, 'All that fighting we did twenty-five years ago. All those dead. Now the Germans are back in France. In two days they'll be here, taking everything we have. Who would have believed it?'

Robbie felt, for the first time, the full ignominy of the retreat.

He was ashamed. He said, with even less conviction than before, 'We'll be back to throw them out, I promise you.'

The brothers nodded, and with final smiles of farewell, left the dim circle of the candle's glow and crossed the darkness towards the open barn door, the glasses chinking against the bottles as they went.

He was woken by a boot nudging the small of his back. 'C'mon, Guv'nor. Rise and shine.'

He sat up and looked at his watch. The barn entrance was a rectangle of bluish black. He had been asleep, he reckoned, for less than forty-five minutes. Mace diligently emptied the straw from the sacks and dismantled his table. They sat in silence on the hay bales smoking the first cigarette of the day. When they stepped outside they found a clay pot with a heavy wooden lid. Inside, wrapped in a muslin cloth, was a loaf and a wedge of cheese. Robbie divided the provisions right there with a bowie knife.

'In case we're separated,' he murmured.

A light was on already in the farmhouse and the dogs were in a frenzy as they walked away. They climbed a gate and began to cross a field in a northerly direction. After an hour they stopped in a coppiced wood to drink from their canteens and smoke. Robbie studied the map. Already, the first bombers were high overhead, a formation of about fifty Heinkels, heading the same way to the coast. The sun was coming up and there was little cloud. A perfect day for the Luftwaffe. They walked in silence for an hour. There was no path, so he made a route by the compass, through fields of cows and sheep, turnips and young wheat. They were not as safe as he thought, away from the road—one field of cattle had a dozen shell craters, and fragments of flesh, bone and brindled skin had been blasted across a hundred yard stretch. But each man was folded into his thoughts and no one spoke. Robbie was troubled by the map. He guessed they were twenty-five miles from Dunkirk. The closer they came, the harder it would be to stay off the roads. Everything converged. There were rivers and canals to cross. When they headed for the bridges they would only lose time if they cut away across country again.

Just after ten they stopped for another rest. They had climbed a fence to reach a track, but he could not find it on the map. It ran in the right direction anyway, over flat, almost treeless land. They had gone another half-hour when they heard anti-aircraft fire a couple of miles ahead where they could see the spire of a church. He stopped to consult the map again.

Corporal Nettle said, 'It don't show crumpet, that map.'

'Ssh. He's having his doubts.'

Robbie leaned his weight against a fence post. His side hurt whenever he put his right foot down. The sharp thing seemed to be protruding and snagging on his shirt. Impossible to resist probing with a forefinger. But he felt only tender, ruptured flesh. After last night, it wasn't right he should have to listen to the corporals' taunts again. Tiredness and pain were making him irritable, but he said nothing and tried to concentrate. He found the village on the map, but not the track, though it surely led there. It was just as he had thought. They would join the road, and they would need to stay on it all the way to the defence line at the Bergues-Furnes canal. There was no other route. The corporals' banter was continuing. He folded the map and walked on.

'What's the plan, Guv'nor?'

He did not reply.

'Oh oh. Now you've offended her.'

Beyond the ack-ack, they heard artillery fire, their own, some way further to the west. As they approached the village they heard the sound of slow-moving lorries. Then they saw them, stretching in a line to the north, travelling at walking pace. It was going to be tempting to hitch a ride, but he knew from experience what an easy target they would be from the air. On foot you could see and hear what was coming.

Their track joined the road where it turned a right-angled corner to leave the village. They rested their feet for ten minutes, sitting on the rim of a stone water trough. Three- and ten-ton lorries, half-tracks and ambulances were grinding round the narrow turn at less than one mile an hour, and moving away from the village down a long straight road whose left side was flanked by plane trees. The road led directly north, towards a black cloud of burning oil that stood above the horizon, marking out Dunkirk. No need for a compass now. Dotted along the way were disabled military vehicles. Nothing was to be left for enemy use. From the backs of receding lorries the conscious wounded stared out blankly. There were also armoured cars, staff cars, Bren gun carriers and motorbikes. Mixed in with them and stuffed or piled high with household gear and suitcases were civilian cars, buses, farm trucks, and carts pushed by men and women or pulled by horses. The air was grey with diesel fumes, and straggling wearily through the stench, and for the moment moving faster than the traffic, were hundred of soldiers, most of them carrying their rifles and their awkward greatcoats—a burden in the morning's growing warmth.

Walking with the soldiers were families carrying suitcases, bundles, babies, or holding the hands of children. The only human sound Robbie heard, piercing the din of engines, was the crying of babies. There were old people walking singly. One old man in a fresh lawn suit, bow tie and carpet slippers shuffled by with the help of two sticks, advancing so slowly that even the traffic was passing him. He was panting hard. Wherever he was going he surely would not make it. On the far side of the road, right on the corner, was a shoe shop open for business. Robbie saw a woman with a little girl at her side talking to a shop assistant who displayed a different shoe in the palm of each hand. The three paid no attention to the procession behind them. Moving against the flow, and now trying to edge round this same corner, was a column of armoured cars, the paintwork untouched by battle, heading south into the German advance. All they could hope to achieve against a Panzer division was an extra hour or two for the retreating soldiers.

Robbie stood up, drank from his canteen and stepped into the procession, slipping in behind a couple of Highland Light Infantry men. The corporals followed him. He no longer felt responsible for them now they had joined the main body of the retreat. His lack of sleep exaggerated his hostility. Today their teasing needled him and seemed to betray the comradeship of the night before. In fact, he felt hostile to everyone around him. His thoughts had shrunk to the small hard point of his own survival. Wanting to shake the corporals off, he quickened his pace, overtook the Scotsmen and pushed his way past a group of nuns shepherding a couple of dozen children in blue tunics. They looked like the rump of a boarding school, like the one he had taught at near Lille in the summer before he went up to

Cambridge. It seemed another man's life to him now. A dead civilization. First his own life ruined, then everybody else's. He strode on angrily, knowing it was a pace he could not maintain for long. He had been in a column like this before, on the first day, and he knew what he was looking for. To his immediate right was a ditch, but it was shallow and exposed. The line of trees was on the other side. He slipped across, in front of a Renault saloon. As he did so the driver leaned on his horn. The deafening noise startled Robbie into a sudden fury. Enough! He leaped back to the driver's door and wrenched it open. Inside was a trim little fellow in a grey suit and fedora, with leather suitcases piled at his side and his family jammed in the back seat. Robbie grabbed the terrified driver by his tie and was ready to smack his stupid face with an open right hand, but another hand, one of some great strength, closed about his wrist.

'That ain't the enemy, Guv'nor.'

Without releasing his grip, Corporal Mace pulled him away. Nettle, who was just behind, kicked the Renault door shut with such ferocity that the wing mirror fell off. The children in blue tunics cheered and clapped.

They crossed to the other side and walked on under the line of trees. The sun was well up now and it was warm, but the shade was not yet over the road. Some of the vehicles lying across the ditches had been shot up in air attacks. Around the abandoned lorries they passed, supplies had been scattered by troops looking for food or drink or petrol. Robbie and the corporals tramped through typewriter-ribbon spools spilling from their boxes, double-entry ledgers, consignments of tin desks and swivel chairs, cooking utensils and engine parts, saddles, stirrups and harnesses, sewing machines, football trophy cups, stackable chairs, and a film projector and petrol generator, both of which someone had wrecked with the crowbar that was lying nearby. They passed an ambulance, half in the ditch with one wheel removed. A brass plaque on the door said, THIS AMBULANCE IS A GIFT OF THE BRITISH RESIDENTS OF BRAZIL.

It was possible, Robbie found, to fall asleep while walking. The roar of lorry engines would be suddenly cut, then his neck muscles relaxed, his head drooped, and he would wake with a start and a swerve to his step. Nettle and Mace were for getting a lift. But he had already told them the day before what he had seen in that first column—twenty men in the back of a three-ton lorry killed with a single bomb. Meanwhile he had cowered in a ditch with his head in a culvert and caught the shrapnel in his side.

'You go ahead,' he said. 'I'm sticking here.'

So the matter was dropped. They wouldn't go without him—he was their lucky ticket.

They came up behind some more HLI men. One of them was playing the bagpipes, prompting the corporals to begin their own nasal whining parodies. Robbie made as if to cross the road.

'If you start a fight, I'm not with you.'

Already a couple of Scots had turned and were muttering to each other.

'It's a braw bricht moonlicht nicht the nicht,' Nettle called out in Cockney. Something awkward might have developed then if they had not heard a pistol shot from up ahead. As they drew level the bagpipes fell silent. In a wide open field the French cavalry had assembled in force and dismounted to form a queue. At the head stood an officer dispatching each horse with a shot to the head, and then moving on down the line. Each man stood to attention by his mount, holding his hat ceremonially against his chest. The horses patiently waited their turn.

This enactment of defeat depressed everyone's spirits further. The corporals had no heart for a tangle with the Scotsmen who could no longer be bothered with them. Five minutes, later they passed five bodies in a ditch, three women, two children. Their suitcases lay around them. One of the women wore carpet slippers, like the man in the lawn suit. Robbie looked away, determined not to be drawn in. If he was going to survive, he had to keep a watch on the sky. He was so tired, he kept forgetting. And it was hot now. Some men were letting their greatcoats drop to the ground. A glorious day. In another time this was what would have been called a glorious day. Their road was on a long slow rise, enough to be a drag on the legs and increase the pain in his side. Each step was a conscious decision. A blister was swelling on his left heel which forced him to walk on the edge of his boot. Without stopping, he took the bread and cheese from his bag, but he was too thirsty to chew. He lit another cigarette to curb his hunger and tried to reduce his task to the basics: you walked across the land until you came to the sea. What could be simpler, once the social element was removed? He was the only man on earth and his purpose was clear. He was walking across the land until he came to the sea. The reality was all too social, he knew; other men were pursuing him, but he had comfort in a pretence, and a rhythm at least for his feet. He walked/across/the land/until/he came/to the sea. A hexameter. Five iambs and an anapaest was the beat he tramped to now.

Another twenty minutes and the road began to level out. Glancing over his shoulder he saw the convoy stretching back down the hill for a mile. Ahead, he could not see the end of it. They crossed a railway line. By his map they were sixteen miles from the canal. They were entering a stretch where the wrecked equipment along the road was more or less continuous. Half a dozen twenty-five pound guns were piled beyond the ditch, as if swept up there by a heavy bulldozer. Up ahead where the land began to drop there was a junction with a back road and some kind of commotion was taking place. There was laughter from the soldiers on foot and raised voices at the road side. As he came up, he saw a major from the Buffs, a pink-faced fellow of the old school, in his forties, shouting and pointing towards a wood that lay about a mile away across two fields. He was pulling men out of the column, or trying to. Most ignored him and kept going, some laughed at him, but a few were intimidated by his rank and had stopped, though he lacked any show of personal authority. They were gathered around him with their rifles, looking uncertain.

'You. Yes, you. You'll do.'

The major's hand was on Robbie's shoulder. He stopped and saluted before he knew what he was doing. The corporals were behind him.

The major had a little toothbrush moustache overhanging small, tight lips that clipped his words briskly. 'We've got Jerry trapped in the woods over there. He must be an advance party. But he's well dug in with a couple of machine guns. We're going to get in there and flush him out.'

Robbie felt the horror chill and weaken his legs. He showed the major his empty palms.

'What with, sir?'

'With cunning and a bit of teamwork.'

How was the fool to be resisted? Robbie was too tired to think, though he knew he wasn't going.

'Now, I've got the remains of two platoons halfway up the eastern...'

Remains was the word that told the story, and prompted Mace, with all his barrack-room skill, to interrupt.

'Beg pardon, sir. Permission to speak.'

'Not granted, corporal.'

'Thank you, sir. Orders is from GHQ. Proceed at haste and speed and celerity, without delay, diversion or divagation to Dunkirk for the purposes of immediate evacuation on account of being 'orribly and onerously overrun from all directions. Sir.'

The major turned and poked his forefinger into Mace's chest.

'Now look here, you. This is our one last chance to show...'

Corporal Nettle said dreamily, 'It was Lord Gort what wrote out that order, sir, and sent it down personally.'

It seemed extraordinary to Robbie that an officer should be addressed this way. And risky too. The major had not grasped that he was being mocked. He seemed to think that it was Robbie who had spoken, for the little speech that followed was addressed to him.

'The retreat is a bloody shambles. For heaven's sake, man. This is your one last good chance to show what we can do when we're decisive and determined. What's more...'

He went on to say a good deal more, but it seemed to Robbie that a muffling silence descended on the bright late morning scene. This time he wasn't asleep. He was looking past the major's shoulder towards the head of the column. Hanging there, a long way off, about thirty feet above the road, warped by the rising heat, was what looked like a plank of wood, suspended horizontally, with a bulge in its centre. The major's words were not reaching him, and nor were his own clear thoughts. The horizontal apparition hovered in the sky without growing larger, and though he was beginning to understand its meaning, it was, as in a dream, impossible to begin to respond or move his limbs. His only action had been to open his mouth, but he could make no sound, and would not have known what to say, even if he could.

Then, precisely at the moment when sound flooded back in, he was able to shout, 'Go!' And he began to run directly towards the nearest cover. It was the vaguest, least soldierly form of advice, but he sensed the corporals not far behind. Dreamlike too was the way he could not move his legs fast enough. It was not pain he felt below his ribs, but something scraping against the bone. He let his greatcoat fall. Fifty yards ahead was a three-ton lorry on its side. That black greasy chassis, that bulbous differential was his only home. He didn't have long to get there. A fighter was strafing the length of the column. The broad spray of fire was advancing up the road at 200 miles an hour, a rattling hail-storm din of cannon rounds hitting metal and glass. No one inside the near stationary vehicles had started to react. Drivers were only just registering the spectacle through their windscreens. They were where he had been seconds before. Men in the backs of the lorries knew nothing. A sergeant stood in the centre of the road and raised his rifle. A woman screamed, and then the fire was upon them just as Robbie threw himself into the shadow of the upended lorry. The steel frame trembled as rounds hit it with the wild rapidity of a drum roll. Then the cannon fire swept on, hurtling down the column, chased by the fighter's roar and the flicker of its shadow. He pressed himself into the darkness of the chassis by the front wheel. Never had sump oil smelled sweeter. Waiting for another plane, he crouched foetally, his arms cradling his head and eyes tight shut, and thought only of survival.

But nothing came. Only the sounds of insects determined on their late spring business, and birdsong resuming after a decent pause. And then, as if taking their cue from the birds, the wounded began to groan and call out, and terrified children began to cry. Someone, as usual, was cursing the RAF. Robbie stood up and was dusting himself down, when Nettle and Mace emerged and together they walked back towards the major who was sitting on the ground. All the colour had gone from his face, and he was nursing his hand.

'Bullet went clean through it,' he said as they came up. 'Jolly lucky really.'

They helped him to his feet and offered to take him over to an ambulance where a RAMC captain and two orderlies were already seeing to the wounded. But he shook his head and stood there unaided. In shock he was talkative and his voice was softer.

'ME 109. Must have been his machine gun. The cannon would have blown my ruddy hand off. Twenty millimetre you know. He must have strayed from his group. Spotted us on his way home and couldn't resist. Can't blame him really. But it means there'll be more of them pretty soon.'

The half-dozen men he had gathered up before had picked themselves and their rifles out of the ditch and were wandering off. The sight of them recalled the major to himself.

'All right, chaps. Form up.'

They seemed quite unable to resist him and formed a line. Trembling a little now, he turned to Robbie.

'And you three. On the double.'

'Actually, old boy, to tell the truth, I think we'd rather not.'

'Oh, I see.' He squinted at Robbie's shoulder, seeming to see there the insignia of senior rank. He gave a good-natured salute with his left hand. 'In that case sir, if you don't mind, we'll be off. Wish us luck.'

'Good luck, Major.'

They watched him march his reluctant detachment away towards the woods where the machine guns waited.

For half an hour the column did not move. Robbie put himself at the disposal of the RAMC captain and helped on the stretcher parties bringing in the wounded, and afterwards finding a place for them on the lorries. There was no sign of the corporals. He fetched and carried supplies from the back of an ambulance. Watching the captain at work, stitching a head wound, Robbie felt the stirrings of his old ambitions. Along their stretch there were five injured and, surprisingly, no one dead, though the sergeant with the rifle was hit in the face and was not expected to live. Three vehicles had their front ends shot up and were pushed off the road. The petrol was siphoned off, and for good measure, bullets were fired through the tyres.

When all this was done in their section, there was still no movement up at the front of the column. Robbie retrieved his greatcoat and walked on. He was too thirsty to wait about. An elderly Belgian lady shot in the knee had drunk the last of his water. His tongue was large in his mouth and all he could think of now was finding a drink. That, and keeping a watch on the sky. He passed sections like his own where vehicles were being disabled and the wounded were being lifted into lorries. He had been going for ten minutes when he saw Mace's head on the grass by a pile of dirt. It was about twenty-five yards away, in the deep green shadow of a stand of poplars. He went towards it, even though he suspected that it would be better for his state of mind to walk on. He found Mace and Nettle shoulder deep in a hole. They were in the final stages of digging a grave. Lying face down beyond the pile of earth was a boy of fifteen or so. A crimson stain on the back of his white shirt spread from neck to waist.

Mace leaned on his shovel and did a passable imitation. '"I think we'd rather not." Very good, Guv'nor. I'll remember that next time.'

'Divagation was nice. Where d'you get that one?'

'He swallowed a fucking dictionary,' Corporal Nettle said proudly.

'I used to like the crossword.'

'And "'orribly and onerously overrun?"'

'That was a concert party they had in the sergeants' mess last Christmas.'

Still in the grave, he and Nettle sang tunelessly for Robbie's benefit.

'Twas ostensibly ominous in the overview
To be 'orribly and onerously overrun.

Behind them the column was beginning to move.

'Better stick him in,' Corporal Mace said.

The three men lifted the boy down and set him on his back. Clipped to his shirt pocket was a row of fountain pens. The corporals didn't pause for ceremony. They began to shovel in the dirt and soon the boy had vanished.

Nettle said, 'Nice looking kid.'

The corporals had bound two tent poles with twine to make a cross. Nettle banged it in with the back of his shovel. As soon as it was done they walked back to the road.

Mace said, 'He was with his grandparents. They didn't want him left in the ditch. I thought they'd come over and see, but they're in a terrible state. We better tell them where he is.'

But the boy's grandparents were not to be seen. As they walked on, Robbie took out the map and said, 'Keep watching the sky.' The major was right—after the Messerschmitt's casual pass, they would be back. They should have been back by now. The Bergues-Furnes canal was marked in thick bright blue on his map. His impatience to reach it had become inseparable from his thirst. He would put his face in that blue and drink deeply. This thought put him in mind of childhood fevers, their wild and frightening logic, the search for the cool corner of the pillow, and his mother's hand upon his brow. Dear Grace. When he touched his own forehead the skin was papery and dry. The inflamation round his wound, he sensed, was growing, and the skin was becoming tighter, harder, with something, not blood, leaking out of it on to his shirt. He wanted to examine himself in private, but that was hardly possible here. The convoy was moving at its old inexorable pace. Their road ran straight to the coast—there would be no short cuts now. As they drew closer, the black cloud, which surely came from a burning refinery in Dunkirk, was beginning to rule the northern sky. There was nothing to do but walk towards it.

There was more confusion ahead, more shouting. Incredibly, an armoured column was forcing its way against the forward press of traffic, soldiers and refugees. The crowd parted reluctantly. People squeezed into the gaps between abandoned vehicles or against shattered walls and doorways. It was a French column, hardly more than a detachment—three armoured cars, two half-tracks and two troop carriers. There was no show of common cause. Among the British troops the view was that the French had let them down. No will to fight for their own country. Irritated at being pushed aside, the Tommies swore, and taunted their allies with shouts of 'Maginot!' For their part, the poilus must have heard rumours of an evacuation. And here they were, being sent to cover the rear. 'Cowards! To the boats! Go shit in your pants!' Then they were gone, and the crowd closed in again under a cloud of diesel smoke and walked on.

They were approaching the last houses in the village. In a field ahead, he saw a farmer and his collie dog walking behind a horse-drawn plough. Like the ladies in the shoe shop, he did not seem aware of the convoy. These lives were lived in parallel—war was a hobby for the enthusiasts and no less serious for that. Like the deadly pursuit of a hunt to hounds, while over the next hedge a woman in the back seat of a passing motor car was absorbed in her knitting, and in the bare garden of a new house a man was teaching his son to kick a ball. Yes, it would still go on and there'd be a crop, someone to reap it and mill it, others to eat it, and not everyone would be dead.

Robbie was thinking this when Nettle gripped his arm and pointed. The commotion of the passing French column had covered the sound, but they were easy enough to see. There were at least fifteen of them, at 10,000 feet, little dots in the blue, circling above the road. Robbie and the corporals stopped to watch, and everyone nearby saw them too.

A voice hoarse with exhaustion murmured close to his ear, 'Fuck. Where's the RAF?'

Another said knowingly, 'They'll go for the Frogs.'

As if goaded into disproof, one of the specks peeled away and began its near vertical dive, directly above their heads. For seconds the sound did not reach them. The silence was building like pressure in their ears. Even the wild shouts that went up and down the road did not relieve it. Take cover! Disperse! Disperse! On the double!

It was difficult to move. He could walk on at a steady trudge, and he could stop, but it was an effort, an effort of memory, to reach for the unfamiliar commands, to turn away from the road and run. They had stopped by the last house in the village. Beyond the house was a barn and flanking both was the field where the farmer had been ploughing. Now he was standing under a tree with his dog, as though sheltering from a shower of rain. His horse, still in harness, grazed along the unploughed strip. Soldiers and civilians were streaming away from the road in all directions. A woman brushed past him carrying a crying child, then she changed her mind and came back and stood, turning indecisively at the side of the road. Which way? The farmyard or the field? Her immobility delivered him from his own. As he pushed her by the shoulder towards the gate, the rising howl commenced. Nightmares had become a science. Someone, a mere human, had taken the time to dream up this satanic howling.

31

And what success! It was the sound of panic itself, mounting and straining towards the extinction they all knew, individually, to be theirs. It was a sound you were obliged to take personally. Robbie guided the woman through the gate. He wanted her to run with him into the centre of the field. He had touched her, and made her decision for her, so now he felt he could not leave her. But the boy was at least six years old and heavy, and together they were making no progress at all. He pulled the child from her arms.

'Come on,' he shouted.

A Stuka carried a single 1,000-ton bomb. The idea was to get away from buildings and other people. The pilot was not going to waste his precious load on a lone figure in a field. If he turned back to strafe it would be another matter. Robbie had seen them hunt down a sprinting man for the sport of it. With a free hand he was dragging on the woman's arm. The boy was screaming in his ear. He was wetting his pants. The mother seemed incapable of running. She was stretching out her hand and shouting. She wanted her son back. The child was wriggling towards her, across his shoulder. Now came the screech of the falling bomb. They said that if you heard the noise stop before the explosion, your time was up. As he dropped to the grass he pulled the woman with him and pushed her head down. He was half lying across the child as the ground shook to the unbelievable roar. The shock wave prised them from the earth. They covered their faces against the stinging spray of dirt. They heard the Stuka climb from its dive even as they heard the banshee wail of the next attack. The bomb had hit the road less than eighty yards away. He had the boy under his arm and he was trying to pull the woman to her feet.

'We've got to run again. We're too close to the road.'

The woman answered but he did not understand her. Again they were stumbling across the field. He felt the pain in his side like a flash of colour. The boy was in his arms, and again the woman seemed to be dragging back, and trying to get her son from him. There were hundreds in the field now, all making for the woods on the far side. At the shrill whine of the bomb everyone cowered on the ground. But the woman had no instinct for danger and he had to pull her down again. This time they were pressing their faces into the freshly turned earth. As the screech grew louder the woman shouted what

1. New American Writing 2. The Portage to San Cristobal of
A.H. 3. The End of the English Novel 4. Beyond the Crisis 5.
The Modern Common Wind 6. A Literature for Politics 7.
Best of Young British Novelists (I) 8. Dirty Realism 9. John
Berger, 'Boris' 10. Travel Writing 11. Milan Kundera:
Greetings from Prague 12. The Rolling Stones 13. After the
Revolution 14. Autobiography 15. James Fenton, 'The Fall
of Saigon' 16. Science 17. Graham Greene,'While Waiting
for a War' 18. James Fenton, 'The Snap Revolution' 19.
More Dirt 20. In Trouble Again: A Special Issue of Travel
Writing 21. The Story-Teller 22. With Your Tongue Down
My Throat 23. Home 24. Inside Intelligence 25. The
Murderee 26. Travel 27. Death 28. Birthday special! 29.
New World 30. New Europe! 31. The General 32. History 33.
What Went Wrong? 34. Death of a Harvard Man 35. The
Unbearable Peace 36. Vargas Llosa 37. The Family 38.
We're So Happy! 39. The Body 40. The Womanizer 41.
Biography 42. Krauts! 43. Best of Young British Novelists
(II) 44. The Last Place on Earth 45. Gazza Agonistes 46.
Crime 47. Losers 48. Africa 49. Money 50. Fifty! 51. Big
Men (and L.A. Women) 52. Food 53. News: Scoops, Lies
and Videotape 54. Best of Young American Novelists 55.
Children: Blind, Bitter Happiness 56. What Happened To
Us? Britain's Valedictory Realism 57. India: the Golden
Jubilee 58. Ambition 59. France 60. Unbelievable: Unlikely
Ends, Fateful Escapes and the Fascism of Flowers 61. The
Sea 62. 63. Beasts 64. Russia: The Wild
East 65. London: The Lives of the City 66. Truth + Lies 67.
Women and Children First 68. Love Stories 69. The
Assassin 70. Australia: The New, New World 71. Shrinks
72. Overreachers 73. Due out March 2001...

Answer overleaf...

sounded like a prayer. He realized then that she wasn't speaking French. The explosion was on the far side of the road, more than a 150 yards away. But now the first Stuka was turning over the village and dropping for the strafe. The boy had gone silent with shock. His mother wouldn't stand. Robbie pointed to the Stuka coming in over the roof tops. They were right in its path and there was no time for argument. She wouldn't move. He threw himself down into the furrow. The rippling thuds of machine-gun fire in the ploughed earth and the engine roar flashed past them. A wounded soldier was screaming. Robbie was on his feet. But the woman would not take his hand. She sat on the ground and hugged the boy tightly to her. She was speaking Flemish to him, soothing him, surely telling him that everything was going to be all right. Mama would see to that. Robbie didn't know a single word of the language. It would have made no difference. She paid him no attention. The boy was staring at him blankly over his mother's shoulder.

Robbie took a step back. Then he turned and ran. As he floundered across the furrows the attack was coming in. The rich soil was clinging to his boots. Only in nightmares were feet so heavy. A bomb fell on the road, way over in the centre of the village, where the lorries were. But one screech hid another, and it hit the field before he could go down. The blast lifted him forwards several feet and drove him face first into the soil. When he came to, his mouth and nose and ears were filled with dirt. He was trying to clear his mouth, but he had no saliva. He used a finger, but that was worse. He was gagging on the dirt, then he was gagging on his filthy finger. He blew the dirt from his nose. His snot was mud and it covered his mouth. But the woods were near, there would be streams and waterfalls and lakes in there. He saw a paradise. When the rising howl of a diving Stuka sounded again, he struggled to place the sound. Was it the all-clear? His thoughts too were clogged. He could not spit or swallow, he could not easily breathe, and he could not think. Then, at the sight of the farmer with his dog still waiting patiently under the tree, it came back to him, he remembered everything and he turned to look back. Where the woman and her son had been was a crater. Even as he saw it, he thought he had always known. That was why he had to leave them. His business was to survive, though he had forgotten why. He kept on towards the woods.

He walked a few steps into the tree cover, and sat in the new undergrowth with his back to a birch sapling. His only thought was of water. There were 200 or so sheltering in the woods, including some wounded who had dragged themselves in. There was a man, a civilian, not far off, crying and shouting in pain. Robbie got up and moved further away. All the new greenery spoke to him only of water. The attack continued on the road and over the village. He cleared away old leaves and used his helmet to dig. The soil was damp but no water oozed into the hole he had made, even when it was eighteen inches deep. So he sat and thought about water and tried to clean his tongue against his sleeve. When a Stuka dived, it was impossible not to tense and shrink, though each time he thought he didn't have the strength. Towards the end they came over to strafe the woods, but to no effect. Leaves and twigs tumbled from the canopy. Then the planes were gone, and in the huge silence that loomed over the fields and trees and the village, there was not even birdsong. After a while, from the direction of the road came blasts of a whistle for the all-clear. But no one moved. He remembered this from last time. They were too dazed, they were in shock from repeated episodes of terror. Each dive brought every man, cornered and cowering, to face his execution. When it did not come, the trial had to be lived through all over again and the fear did not diminish. For the living, the end of a Stuka attack was the paralysis of shock, of repeated shocks. The sergeants and junior officers might come around shouting and kicking the men into standing. But they were drained, and for a good while, useless as troops.

So he sat there in a daze like everyone else, just as he had the first time, outside the village whose name he could not remember. These French villages with Belgian names. When he was separated from his unit, and what was worse, for an infantryman, from his rifle. How many days ago? There could be no way of knowing. He examined his revolver which was clogged with dirt. He removed the ammunition and tossed the gun into the bushes. After a time there was a sound behind him and a hand was on his shoulder.

'Here you go. Courtesy of the Green Howards.'

Corporal Mace gave him the dead man's water bottle. Since it was almost full he used the first swig to rinse out his mouth, but that was a waste. He drank the dirt with the rest.

'Mace, you're an angel.'

The corporal extended a hand to pull him up. 'Got to shift. There's a rumour the fucking Belgians have collapsed. We might get cut off from the east. Still miles to go.'

As they were walking back across the field, Nettle joined them. He had a bottle of wine which they passed around.

'Nice bouquet,' Robbie said.

'Dead Frog.'

The peasant and his collie were back behind the plough. The three soldiers approached the crater where the smell of cordite was strong. The hole was a perfectly symmetrical inverted cone whose sides were smooth, as though finely raked. There were no human signs, not a shred of clothing or shoe leather. Mother and child had been vaporized. He paused to absorb this fact, but the corporals were in a hurry and pushed him on and soon they joined the stragglers on the road.

It was in his clear moments he was troubled. It wasn't the wound, though it hurt at every step, and it wasn't the dive-bombers circling over the beach some miles to the north. It was his mind. Periodically, something slipped. Some everyday principle of continuity, the humdrum element that told him where he was in his own story, faded from his use, abandoning him to a waking dream in which there were thoughts, but no sense of who was having them. No responsibility, no memory of the hours before, no idea of what he was about, where he was going, what his plan was. And no curiosity about these matters. He would then find himself in the grip of illogical certainties.

He was in this state as they came round the eastern edge of the resort of Bray Dunes after three hours' walking. They went down a street of shattered glass and broken roof tiles where children were playing and watching the soldiers go by. Nettle had put his boots back on, but he had left them loose, with the laces trailing. Suddenly, like a jack-in-a-box, a lieutenant from the Dorsets popped up from the cellar of a municipal building taken over for a headquarters. He came towards them at a self-important clip with an attaché case under his arm. When he stopped in front of them they saluted. Scandalized, he ordered the corporal to tie his laces immediately or face a charge.

While the corporal knelt to obey, the lieutenant—round-shouldered, bony, with a desk-bound look and a wisp of ginger moustache—said, 'You're a bloody disgrace, man.'

In the lucid freedom of his dream state, Robbie intended to shoot the officer through the chest. It would be better for everybody. It was hardly worth discussing the matter in advance. He reached for it, but his gun had gone—he couldn't remember where—and the lieutenant was already walking away.

After minutes of noisy crunching over glass, there was sudden silence under their boots where the road ended in fine sand. As they rose through a gap in the dunes, they heard the sea and tasted a salty mouthful before they saw it. The taste of holidays. They left the path and climbed through the dune grass to a vantage point where they stood in silence for many minutes. The fresh damp breeze off the Channel restored him to clarity. Perhaps it was nothing more than his temperature rising and falling in fits.

He thought he had no expectations—until he saw the beach. He'd assumed that the cussed spirit which abhorred, in the face of annihilation, untied laces would prevail on the beach. He tried to impose order now on the random movement before him, and almost succeeded: marshalling centres, warrant officers behind makeshift desks, rubber stamps and dockets, roped-off lines towards the waiting boats; hectoring sergeants, tedious queues around mobile canteens. In general, an end to all private initiative. Without knowing it, that was the beach he had been walking to for days. But the actual beach, the one he and the corporals gazed on now, was no more than a variation on all that had gone before: there was a rout, and this was its terminus. It was obvious enough now they saw it—this was what happened when a chaotic retreat could go no further. It only took a moment to adjust. He saw thousands of men, 10,000, 20,000, perhaps more, spread across the vastness of the beach. In the distance they were like grains of black sand. But there were no boats, apart from one upturned whaler rolling in the distant surf. It was low tide and almost a mile to the water's edge. There were no boats by the long jetty. He blinked and looked again. That jetty was made of men, a long file of them, six or eight deep, standing up to their knees, their waists, their shoulders, stretching out for 500 yards through the shallow waters. They waited, but there was nothing in sight, unless you counted in those smudges on the horizon—boats burning after an air attack. There was nothing that could reach the beach in hours. But the troops stood there, facing the horizon in their tin hats, rifles lifted above the waves. From this distance they looked as placid as cattle.

And these men were a small proportion of the total. The majority were on the beach, moving about aimlessly. Little clusters had formed around the wounded left by the last Stuka attack. As aimless as the men, half a dozen artillery horses galloped in a pack along the water's edge. A few troops were attempting to right the upturned whaler. Some had taken off their clothes to swim. Off to the east was a football game, and from the same direction came the feeble sound of a hymn being sung in unison, then fading. Beyond the football game was the only sign of official activity. On the shore, lorries were being lined up and lashed together to form a makeshift jetty. More lorries were driving down. Nearer, up the beach, individuals were scooping sand with their helmets to make foxholes. In the dunes, close to where Robbie and the corporals stood, men had already dug themselves holes from which they peeped out, proprietorial and smug. Like marmosets, he thought. But the majority of the army wandered about the sands without purpose, like citizens of an Italian town in the hour of the *passeggio*. They saw no immediate reason to join the enormous queue, but they were unwilling to come away from the beach in case a boat should suddenly appear.

To the left was the resort of Bray, a cheerful front of cafes and little shops that in a normal season would be renting out beach chairs and pedal bikes. In a circular park with a neatly mowed lawn was a bandstand, and a merry-go-round painted red, white and blue. In this setting, another, more insouciant company had hunkered down. Soldiers had opened up the cafes for themselves and were getting drunk at the tables outside, bawling and laughing. Men were larking about on the pedal bikes along a pavement stained with vomit. A colony of drunks was spread out on the grass by the bandstand, sleeping it off. A solitary sunbather in his underpants, face down on a towel, had patches of uneven sunburn on his shoulders and legs— pink and white like a strawberry and vanilla ice cream.

It was not difficult to choose between these circles of suffering— the sea, the beach, the front. The corporals were already walking away. Thirst alone decided it. They found a path on the landward side of the dunes, then they were crossing a sandy lawn strewn with broken bottles. As they were making a way round the raucous tables Robbie saw a naval party coming along the front and stopped to watch them. There were five of them, two officers, three ratings, a gleaming group of fresh white, blue and gold. No concessions to camouflage. Straight-backed and severe, revolvers strapped to their belts, they moved with tranquil authority through the mass of sombre battledress and grimy faces, looking from side to side as if conducting a count. One of the officers made notes on a clipboard. They headed away towards the beach. With a childish feeling of abandonment, Robbie watched them until they were out of sight.

He followed Mace and Nettle into the din and fumy stench of the first bar along the front. Two suitcases propped open on the bar were full of cigarettes—but there was nothing to drink. The shelves along the sandblasted mirror behind the bar were empty. When Nettle ducked behind the counter to rummage around, there were jeers. Everyone coming in had tried the same. The drink had long gone with the serious drinkers outside. Robbie pushed through the crowd to a small kitchen at the back. The place was wrecked, the taps were dry. Outside was a pissoir and stacked crates of empties. A dog was trying to get its tongue inside an empty sardine can, pushing it across a patch of concrete. He turned and went back to the main room and its roar of voices. There was no electricity, only natural light which was stained brown, as though by the absent beer. Nothing to drink, but the bar remained full. Men came in, were disappointed and yet they stayed, held there by free cigarettes and the evidence of recent booze. The dispensers dangled empty on the wall where the inverted bottles had been wrenched away. The sweet smell of liquor rose from the sticky cement floor. The noise and press of bodies and damp tobacco air satisfied a homesick yearning for a Saturday night pub. This was the Mile End Road, and Sauchiehall Street, and everywhere in between.

He stood in the din, uncertain what to do. It would be such an effort, to fight his way out of the crowd. There were boats yesterday, he gathered from a snatch of conversation, and perhaps again tomorrow. Standing on tiptoe by the kitchen doorway, he gave a no-luck shrug across the crowd towards the corporals. Nettle cocked his head in the direction of the door and they began to converge on it. A drink would have been fine, but what interested them now was water. Progress through the press of bodies was slow, and then, just as they converged, their way to the door was blocked by a tight wall of backs forming around one man.

He must have been short—less than five foot six—and Robbie could see nothing of him apart from a portion of the back of his head. Someone said, 'You answer the fucking question, you little git.'

'Yeah, go on then.'

'Where was ya?'

'Where were you when they killed my mate?'

A globule of spittle hit the back of the man's head and fell behind his ear. Robbie moved round to get a view. He saw first the grey-blue of a jacket, and then the mute apprehension in the man's face. He was a wiry little fellow with thick, unclean lenses in his glasses which magnified his frightened stare. He looked like a filing clerk, or a telephone operator, perhaps from a headquarters long ago dispersed. But he was in the RAF and the Tommies held him accountable. He turned slowly, gazing at the circle of his interrogators. He had no answers to their questions, and he made no attempt to deny his responsibility for the absence of Spitfires and Hurricanes over the beach. His right hand clutched his beret so hard his knuckles trembled. An artillery man standing by the door gave him a hard push in the back so that he stumbled across the ring into the chest of a soldier who sent him back with a casual punch to the head. There was a hum of approval. Everyone had suffered, and now someone was going to pay.

'So where's the RAF?'

A hand whipped out and slapped the man's face, knocking his glasses to the floor. The sound of the blow was precise as a whip crack. It was a signal for a new stage, a new level of engagement. His naked eyes shrank to fluttering little dots as he went down to

Ian McEwan

grope around his feet. That was a mistake. A kick from a steel-capped army boot caught him on the backside, lifting him an inch or two. There were chuckles all round. A sense of something tasty about to happen was spreading across the bar and drawing more soldiers in. As the crowd swelled around the circle, any remaining sense of individual responsibility fell away. A swaggering recklessness was taking hold. A cheer went up as someone stubbed his cigarette on the fellow's head. They laughed at his comic yelp. No one doubted that they hated him and that he deserved everything that was coming his way. He was answerable for the Luftwaffe's freedom of the skies, for every Stuka attack, every dead friend. His slight frame contained every cause of an army's defeat. Robbie assumed there was nothing he could do to help the man without risking a lynching himself. But it was impossible to do nothing. Joining in would be better than nothing. Unpleasantly excited, he strained forward. Now, a tripping Welsh accent proposed the question.

'Where's the RAF?'

It was eerie that the man had not shouted for help, or pleaded, or protested his innocence. His silence seemed like collusion in his fate. Was he so dim that it had not occurred to him that he might be about to die? Sensibly, he had folded his glasses into his pocket. Without them his face was empty. Like a mole in bright light, he peered around at his tormentors, his lips parted, more in disbelief than in an attempt to form a word. Because he could not see it coming, he took a blow to the face full on. It was a fist this time. As his head flipped back, another boot cracked into his shin and a little sporting cheer went up, with some uneven applause, as though for a decent catch in the slips on the village green. It was madness to go to the man's defence, it was loathsome not to. At the same time, Robbie understood the exhilaration among the tormentors and the insidious way it could claim him. He himself could do something outrageous with his bowie knife and earn the love of a hundred men. To distance the thought he made himself count the two or three soldiers in the circle he reckoned bigger or stronger than himself. But the real danger came from the mob itself, its righteous state of mind. It would not be denied its pleasures.

A situation had now been reached in which whoever threw the

next hit had to earn general approval by being ingenious or funny. There was an eagerness in the air to please by being creative. No one wanted to strike a false note. For a few seconds these conditions imposed restraint. And at some point soon, Robbie knew from his Wandsworth days, the single blow would become a cascade. Then there would be no turning back, and for the RAF man, only one end. A pink blotch had formed on the cheekbone under his right eye. He had drawn his fists up under his chin—he was still gripping his beret—and his shoulders were hunched. It may have been a protective stance, but it was also a gesture of weakness and submission which was bound to provoke greater violence. If he had said something, anything at all, the troops surrounding him might have remembered that he was a man, not a rabbit to be skinned. The Welshman who had spoken was a short, thickset fellow from the sappers. He now produced a belt of canvas webbing and held it up.

'What do you think, lads?'

His precise, insinuating delivery suggested horrors that Robbie could not immediately grasp. Now was his last chance to act. As he looked around for the corporals, there was a roar from close by, like the bellowing of a speared bull. The crowd swayed and stumbled as Mace barged through them into the circle. With a wild hollering yodelling sound, like Johnny Weissmuller's Tarzan, he picked up the clerk from behind in a bear hug, lifting him eighteen inches clear of the ground and shook him from side to side. There were cheers and whistles, foot stamping and wild-west whoops.

'I know what I want to do with him,' Mace boomed. 'I want to drown him in the bloody sea!'

In response, there rose another storm of hooting and stamping. Nettle was suddenly at Robbie's side and they exchanged a look. They guessed what Mace was about and they began to move towards the door, knowing they would have to be quick. Not everyone was in favour of the drowning idea. Even in the frenzy of the moment, some could still recall that the tideline was a mile away across the sands. The Welshman in particular felt cheated. He was holding up his webbing and shouting. There were catcalls and boos as well as cheers. Still holding his victim in his arms, Mace rushed for the door. Robbie and Nettle were ahead of him, making a path through the crowd. When they reached the entrance—usefully, a single, not a double door—they let Mace through, then they blocked the way, shoulder to shoulder, though they appeared not to, for they were shouting and shaking their fists like the rest. They felt against their backs a colossal and excited human weight which they could only resist for a matter of seconds. This was long enough for Mace to run, not towards the sea, but sharp left, and left again, up a narrow street that curved behind the shops and bars, away from the front.

The exultant crowd exploded from the bar like champagne, hurling Robbie and Nettle aside. Someone thought he saw Mace down on the sands, and for half a minute the crowd went that way. By the time the mistake was realized and the crowd began to turn back, there was no sign of Mace and his man. Robbie and Nettle had melted away too.

The vast beach, the thousands waiting on it, and the sea empty of boats returned the Tommies to their predicament. They emerged from a dream. Away to the east where the night was rising, the perimeter line was under heavy artillery fire. The enemy was closing in and England was a long way off. In the failing light not much time remained to find somewhere to bed down. A cold wind was rising off the Channel, and the greatcoats lay on the road sides far inland. The crowd began to break up. The RAF man was forgotten.   □

YANGDOL'S
JOURNEY

PHOTOGRAPHS AND TEXT BY MANUEL BAUER

On 19 December 1996, Deyang, a thirteen-year-old Tibetan girl, whose name means 'Melodious Happiness', died from exposure while she was trying to cross the Himalayas to Nepal. It was her third attempt and the first time she had reached the border with Nepal. A week later, a thirteen-year-old Tibetan boy died of frostbite in hospital in Kathmandu, after making the same journey. In November 1998, Chinese police shot a fifteen-year-old Tibetan boy near the Nepalese border. He died in hospital from his wounds. All three had belonged to groups of Tibetan refugees attempting to escape Chinese rule at home and cross the border into Nepal.

Every year, more than 2,000 Tibetan refugees arrive in Nepal and India seeking asylum. Almost fifty per cent of them are children. The majority are unaccompanied by their parents but trusted to guides and other refugees who it is hoped will deliver them into the care of the Tibetan authorities in exile. If they are caught by Chinese border patrols, they will be returned to Tibet where they run the risk of detention or imprisonment.

Thousands of children have left Tibet this way since the Chinese occupation in the 1950s. Once in India, many of them have been educated in one of the network of Tibetan schools where they can continue their traditional Tibetan schooling, which is restricted under the system of 'patriotic education' imposed on secondary schools throughout China and Tibet. The Tibetan nation in exile has its capital in Dharamsala, India, where the Fourteenth Dalai Lama, who made his own escape from Tibet in 1959, has his headquarters, and where his sister runs one of several schools for Tibetan children.

In 1995, the Swiss photographer Manuel Bauer made contact with a Tibetan who was planning to take his six-year-old daughter across the Himalayas on foot. He agreed to let Bauer, who is also a mountaineer, go with them. What follows are extracts from the diary he kept on the journey.

Day one: I am sitting in my hotel room in Lhasa having just come back from Bayi, a major Han Chinese military base in central Tibet. 'Bayi' stands for August 1, the day the People's Liberation Army was founded in 1927. In that sprawling concrete city it was all too clear how hopeless it is for Tibetans to retain their cultural identity inside

Previous page: Tibetan pilgrims prostrate themselves on one of the holy routes encircling the city of Lhasa as Chinese troops pass by. Above: the military base at Bayi. Below: Tibetans selling scraps of cloth in the street.

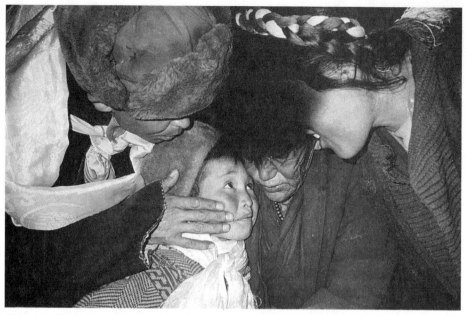

Above: Yangdol parting from her mother and grandmother. If they reach India her father plans to enrol her in boarding school in Dharamsala. Below: the first day: the two leave Lhasa on the back of a truck.

their own country. In Lhasa the Chinese are clearly favoured with better schools and housing and higher incomes.

Day three: I have been put in contact with a Tibetan who plans to escort his daughter into exile in India. My idea, which I've carried around with me for five years now, is finally coming to life.

Day four: I had my first meeting with Kelsang at one of the Chinese shopping centres in Lhasa. He was looking for shoes for the trip. It's important to have strong footwear in order to avoid frostbite and possibly having your feet amputated at the end of the journey. He rejected a sturdy looking pair of boots which turned out to have cardboard soles, and bought two pairs of sneakers, which are lightweight and reasonably durable.

Day seven: Kelsang took me to meet his family in the old part of the city. We went at night. The streets were empty. The clocks in Lhasa are adjusted to Chinese time and the Chinese go to bed early. His wife and mother welcomed me with some suspicion. A small girl came into the room carrying a tray with cups of butter tea. This was Yangdol. I wondered if she had any idea what was in store for her. With gestures her parents explained to me that they were putting all their hopes on the little girl to continue their traditions outside Tibet.

Day nine: I have adopted the guise of an antiques dealer. Kelsang is a carpenter and this way my visits to him won't arouse suspicion. The Chinese don't want negative press from inside Tibet, so contact with foreigners is heavily restricted. Late this evening, Kelsang knocked on my door. He was a bit tipsy. He had persuaded a higher official to issue him and his daughter with a travel permit for a pilgrimage to Lake Manasarovar. It took him quite a lot of drinking and some extra money, but it worked. I got myself a permit for the road to Kathmandu, which should cover the first part of the trip.

Day ten: We left Lhasa this morning on the back of a truck. At nightfall, at our first stop, we were told we would have to wait for a few days because of bad weather. This year the snowy season extended a long way into spring. Yangdol and Kelsang used the time to pray for the success of their journey at a nearby monastery. I decided to prepare myself by climbing the surrounding hills. I watched vultures circling a Tibetan burial ground. The Tibetans cut their dead into pieces and leave them out in the open air, so the body can complete the cycle of life in harmony with the laws of nature.

Day fifteen: My only contact with Kelsang for the last couple of days has been signs in the dust on the side of the hotel telling me each time the trip has been postponed for another day. The clerks at the hotel are getting suspicious about me.

Day seventeen: We finally set off again by truck and reached the foot of the Himalayas. We can see Everest and Cho Oyu, both over 8,000 metres, high in the distance.

Day eighteen: This morning we hitched a ride which took us into the vast plateau. We passed a military camp on the outskirts of a small town and decided to continue on foot. We were very conspicuous; a military jeep could have picked us up at any time. At the sight of any moving object we threw ourselves into one of the small dips in the ground. Luckily, the objects turned out to be yaks or shepherds. We crossed frozen rivers, the ice cracking beneath our feet. In the evening we stopped at a small village. The village head was disturbed by my presence and took our permits to be checked overnight. We lodged with a local family. Yangdol made friends with the cat.

Day nineteen: We hired a pony cart and driver for the first pass. Stopping for a break, we ate dried goat's meat and *tsampa*, the Tibetans' staple food of roasted barley flour. The cart owner offered us *tschang*, traditional beer from the Himalayas. Eventually a collapsed bridge meant we had to go ahead on foot through this high-altitude stone desert. One slip could have meant a twisted ankle and the end of the trip. We had to move quickly because the area was heavily patrolled by border guards, and a strong headwind forced us to keep close to the ground so we wouldn't be swept off

Above: crossing the frozen tundra is dangerous for the refugees since they can be easily spotted by Chinese military patrols. Below: the Himalayas far ahead; Yangdol and her father will soon have to continue on foot.

Above: Kelsang smears yak butter on Yangdol's face as protection from the cutting mountain cross-winds.
Below: frostbite and the amputation of toes and feet is one of the greatest hazards of the mountain passage.

our feet. By sunset we reached a group of stone walls about two feet high built as a windbreak.We decided to spend the night there and crammed ourselves into my one-man tent.

Day twenty: Today the weather was fair, but the wind was still strong. Yangdol doesn't look as happy as she did three days ago. At this altitude one has to drink at least five litres a day to avoid dehydration. Water has become our major problem. My camping stove won't work due to lack of oxygen and the plastic bags holding drinking water are frozen. I had expected to travel with a larger group who would have been more organized, but now we three have to depend on each other to survive.

Day twenty-one: This morning Kelsang had to carry Yangdol on his back. She was freezing. The wind picked up and it was snowing, which reduced our vision and meant we had to move more slowly. At noon, as we reached the first glacier, the sun came out. Yangdol walked by her father's side. He has smeared her face with yak butter to protect her from the sun. The twenty minutes we needed to pack our belongings proved fatal to our feet, even rubbing didn't bring them back to life. The air is getting thinner and we have to make frequent halts to catch our breath. But at least the wind isn't strong enough to blow the snow particles into our faces, otherwise, like other refugees have done, we would die of suffocation.

Suddenly we saw three small dots coming down the pass. They turned out to be a group of smugglers returning from Nepal. Kelsang asked them about conditions up ahead. They reassured us we wouldn't be running into bad weather

Finally, thirsty, hungry and with frozen feet, we reached the top of the pass and the border with Nepal. Kelsang screamed '*Lha Gyallo!*' into the icy wind, which means 'Victory to the gods'. He placed a *khata*, a white scarf, on the altar of piled-up stones. A huge desert of snow and ice stretched before us. On the way down, Yangdol slipped and skidded along the ice luckily coming to a halt at a small rise. She seemed to have sprained her ankle, but refused to let her father carry her. As we walked on in the twilight, it began to snow. Finally, in the light of my small torch, we came to what

appeared to be a group of small stables. Very badly dehydrated, exhausted and almost delirious, we fell asleep.

Day twenty-two: I woke up freezing. Outside the snow had stopped. We dug a small hole and found water in the bottom. In the afternoon we met a shepherd and his son who told us there was a border patrol in the next village. We made our way slowly along the banks of a river in the darkness. Kelsang turned Yangdol's jacket inside out so she wouldn't be so conspicuous. Suddenly a spotlight shone in our direction. We ducked behind a low wall. We were lucky. We hadn't expected a border patrol this early. We crossed the river and looked for a hiding place for the night.

Day twenty-four: We rose with the sun this morning and descended through a heavily wooded area to a popular tourist base for trekking in the mountains. We stopped at a local monastery, where Yangdol was given a bath and inspected for fleas by one of the nuns.

Day twenty-five: Yangdol's ankle hurts and is still swollen. She won't be able to make the twelve-day journey to Kathmandu on foot, so Kelsang has decided to go by helicopter. Since refugees are not allowed to buy tickets, I asked for three, one for myself and two for my Nepalese guides. We go the day after tomorrow, so we can rest.

Day twenty-six: The flight was postponed. Back at the hotel, Kelsang ordered a bottle of whisky and took it upstairs. I wondered why he needed a drink so badly. I went up after him. When he took off his shoes, I realized what the problem was. One of his toes was frozen black. He was going to amputate it because of the pain and the risk of infection. Tears and sweat ran down his face as I held him in my arms. I persuaded him to wait while I found some painkillers. Gradually he calmed down and decided against such a drastic measure.

Day twenty-seven: The helicopter finally arrived and an hour later we landed in Kathmandu. The Tibetans in exile have built up a good infrastructure for refugees in Nepal and India. There are reception centres in both countries where Tibetans are given vaccinations,

Previous pages: Kelsang and Yangdol reach the altar marking the border with Nepal, where they offer prayers to the gods, then begin their descent. Below: after two days without water, drinking from a frozen lake.

Above: after walking for sixteen hours the day before, Yangdol and her father shelter in a monastery where the nuns give her a bath and wash her hair. Below: arriving in Kathmandu after their journey by helicopter.

Above: the reception centre in Kathmandu registers incoming refugees and the UNHCR issues papers for entry into India. Below: in Dharamsala, Yangdol waits in the rain for her first glimpse of the Dalai Lama.

Above: the Dalai Lama greets Yangdol at his headquarters-in-exile in Dharamsala and gives her his blessing. Below: she is one of hundreds of children who arrive every year to be educated at Tibetan schools in India.

official papers and financial aid to pay for the trip to Dharamsala. The UNHCR supports the reception centres and issues the necessary permits for entry into India. But there is always the risk of Nepalese officials deporting Tibetan refugees back across the Chinese border.

Day thirty: We arrived by bus in Delhi on our way to Dharamsala. The bus was so overcrowded that the border patrol didn't check everyone's papers, including mine. But they did charge an extra 'border fee' for Tibetan-looking passengers, who had no choice but to pay. There were so many stops by different police blocks, all demanding 'fees', that on the outskirts of the city we got off the bus and took a rickshaw to the Tibetan refugee centre. Yangdol isn't used to the climate of the Ganges plain and her face and body have swollen from the humidity and insect bites.

Day thirty-one: This morning Kelsang and Yangdol were registered again and given money for the trip to Dharamsala. We got there early in the morning, in pouring rain, and made our way straight to the Tibetan Institute of Performing Arts, where the Dalai Lama was expected. We queued in our wet clothes, until, for the first time in her life, Yangdol saw the Dalai Lama in the flesh.

Day thirty-two: About fifty newly arrived refugees were sitting on the floor of the reception room waiting for an audience with the Dalai Lama, Kelsang and Yangdol among them. When he arrived, they couldn't hold back their tears. The Dalai Lama talked to everybody about their future in exile, and asked questions about the current situation in Tibet. Before he left everyone received a blessing.

Three days later Yangdol was entered into the boarding school in Dharamsala run by the sister of the Dalai Lama where she is one of 2,500 refugee children learning Tibetan, English, Hindi and the local dialect. As soon as he had settled her into the school, Yangdol's father said his farewells. She has not seen him since. Soon after she arrived in Dharamsala, however, Yangdol discovered that she had an aunt living in India, who has taken Yangdol to her home in the holidays, and visits her in school.

63

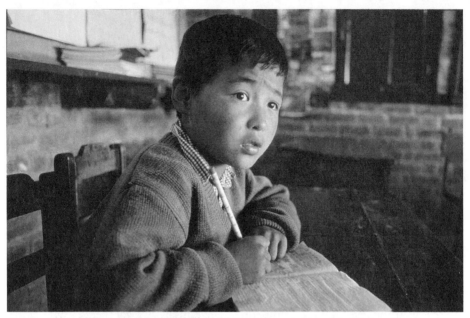

Above and below: five years later, Yangdol is one of 2,500 children studying at the Tibetan school in Dharamsala run by the sister of the Dalai Lama. She learns Tibetan, English, Hindi and the local dialect.

Above and below: Manuel Bauer has returned regularly to Dharamsala to follow Yangdol's progress. She is one of a new generation of children-in-exile keeping Tibetan traditions and Buddhism alive outside Tibet.

Manuel Bauer has been back to see Yangdol in Dharamsala almost every year since 1995. He follows her progress and sometimes photographs her. When she has finished school in Dharamsala, like many of her fellow students, she will have the chance to travel abroad to study, particularly in the United States or Europe, where there are sponsorship schemes to support Tibetan students in exile. After that, there are several options: to work abroad; to return to India to work within the Tibetan administration there, or—and this is the most difficult—to go back to Tibet and work among her own people.

Many returning exiles have found employment as guides working for the travel agencies in Tibet which cater to Western tourists—who prefer Tibetan guides. But recently the Chinese have been recruiting more Chinese tour guides. They believe the Tibetan guides represent a 'security risk', since they talk to Western tourists about their culture and their history. According to the Tibetan Information Network, which monitors the situation inside Tibet, tour guides now have to swear to 'avoid undermining the interests of the country and honour of the nationality either through action or irresponsible talk'.

Since the escape last year of the Seventeenth Karmapa, the fifteen-year-old spiritual head of the Karma Kagyu school of Tibetan Buddhism, who arrived in Dharamsala on January 5, 2000, the Chinese have been instructed to step up their border patrols and have succeeded in intercepting many returning exiles who have been detained by the Chinese authorities.

The most recent threat to the cultural autonomy of the Tibetans, though, comes from the the proposed railway which the Chinese are planning to build linking Lhasa to the main Chinese network in Qinghai province. The Chinese want to exploit the mineral resources and to open up commercial opportunities in Tibet. But it will mean that many more Chinese—civilians, troops and government officials—can travel easily into Tibet, further threatening the Tibetans' traditional way of life, their religion, and further integrating Tibet into the Chinese state. □

Sources: Tibetan Information Network, www.tibetinfo.net

THE 12.10
TO LEEDS
Ian Jack

The Australian writer, Murray Sayle, used to remark when he worked long ago at the London Sunday Times *that a good newspaper story can be of two kinds. One, arrow points to defective part. Two, we name the guilty men. The first has always been easier than the second.*

1. Howe Dell

About sixteen miles north of central London, just before the town of Hatfield, Hertfordshire, there is a small wooded valley with a stream and a pond at the bottom: Howe Dell. This is an ancient place. Flints attributed to the Mesolithic Age have been found at the stream's bottom. Before the English Reformation the church owned the land— it was the Hatfield Rectory's glebe land—until Henry VIII, who was between third and fourth wives at the time, 'conveyed' it along with the Manor of Hatfield to his growing list of property in 1538. Later in the sixteenth century, it was also at Hatfield, at Hatfield House, that Elizabeth Tudor received the news that she was to be queen.

This information can be read on a sign in the dell, which now has the status of 'a valuable urban wildlife site', houses having been built around three sides of it as Hatfield grew from a village to one of London's outer suburbs. Hornbeam, ash, oak and willow grow in the valley; also carpets of bluebells and dog's mercury—though of course no flowers were visible when I went there last December, nor any of the wrens, chaffinches or blue tits which the sign says haunt Howe Dell. It was a grey afternoon; bare trees, earth sodden from the wettest English autumn since 1727, the year that the keeping of records began. Men from the local housing estates walked their dogs through clinging mud. Electric trains passed close by with their windows lit—dinky little reading lights in the first-class carriages of the expresses—but they travelled slowly.

The railway forms the fourth side of Howe Dell, its eastern and most definite boundary, with a high steel fence to keep out people who might damage the railway or get themselves killed. The tracks of the main line from London King's Cross to the north of England and to Scotland curve here, perhaps because the engineers who surveyed the route in the late 1840s wanted to avoid the cost of embankments and bridges over Howe Dell, or because the landowner was stubborn, or because the Great Northern Railway wanted Hatfield's station to be

POPPERFOTO

69

located in the village rather an inconvenient mile outside it. Whatever the cause, the four tracks coming down from London bend to the right and east—a gentle enough curve which trains had safely negotiated for 150 years, until October 17, 2000.

On that day at 12.23 p.m. the 12.10 King's Cross to Leeds express entered the curve at 115 miles an hour—the maximum permitted speed for this stretch of track—and came off the rails. Four people died. They were:

Robert Alcorn, aged thirty-seven, a pilot from New Zealand who had been living in London and was travelling to Leeds to fly a Learjet from there to Jersey;

Steve Arthur, aged forty-six and Alcorn's employer as the owner of the Atlantic Gulf Aviation Company, married with two children aged eight and four, of Pease Pottage, West Sussex;

Leslie Gray, aged forty-three, a solicitor, of Tuxford, Nottinghamshire;

Peter Monkhouse, aged fifty, managing director of an advertising company and returning from a meeting in London, married with three children aged twenty-six, twenty-three and fifteen, of Headingley, Leeds.

All four men had been in the buffet car (coach G). Its roof was ripped off when it struck one of the steel stanchions placed regularly at the side of the track to support the line's overhead electric wires. Another seven coaches were derailed; the locomotive and the first two coaches remained on the track. If the same number of dead had been recorded in a motorway accident, it would have been a small news item. It threatened no record in recent British railway crashes (Southall, 1997, seven dead; Ladbroke Grove, 1999, thirty-one dead). Historical comparison made it almost a minor incident (the three-train Quintinshill collision, 1915, 227 dead). But no other railway accident in British history—or, I would guess, any other country's history—has led to the degree of public anger, managerial panic, political confusion, blame and counter-blame that came in the wake of the Hatfield crash. In fact, outside wars and nuclear accidents, it is hard to think of any technological failure which has had such lasting and widespread effects (to those not directly involved, those not struggling for life in the Atlantic or bereaved on land, the *Titanic* was simply a very thrilling story, a chilling entertainment; *Challenger* halted only a space programme). A week or so later, when overfilled rivers began to flood low-lying England and the first people were emptied from their sandbagged homes into boats, the unsettling impression grew of Britain as an unsound country, weakly equipped, under-skilled, easily made chaotic and only superficially modern; an incompetent society. 'We must be the laughing stock of Europe,' people said (and may have been correct). The reason was elementary: movement. People could not move, in an economy—the world's fourth or fifth largest—which depended on millions of everyday, necessary journeys. Few trains ran; those that did ran unreliably, even to the revised schedules that sometimes doubled or trebled the normal journey times. Travellers tried other methods; motorways became impassable, domestic flights overbooked. At railway stations, even aboard a train itself, would-be passengers were advised to travel 'only if your journey is really necessary'; the train may depart, but it may not arrive—nothing could be guaranteed. In any case, what was necessity, how were we to rank it? Arriving at the office? Reaching a funeral? Getting home? The question hadn't been asked in Britain since the belt-tightening poster campaigns (*Is Your Journey Really Necessary?*) of the Second World War. People old enough to remember the Second World War, its long trains packed with troops crawling through blackouts and air raids, compared that period favourably with the present. There was an enemy then; Britain was a more capable nation.

Two months after the crash, as I walked around Howe Dell, none of this had abated. Every day the newspapers reported a new crisis of trust and confidence in the railways and the businesses which own them (NEW RAIL HORROR: MY JOURNEY TO HELL). I expected to find cut flowers at the site—the 'floral tributes' which mark the place of death by accident or murder on many British streets; bouquets tied to lamp posts and the flashing beacons at pedestrian crossings (there were 3,423 deaths on British roads and thirty-three on railways in 1999). I wanted, I suppose, some bitter monument, the names of the dead attached to a slogan—*Killed by Stubborn Political Ideology*, maybe, or *They Died in the Cause of Profit*—something to set against the sweetness of the wild-flower information of the sign across the stream in the woods. But other than the mud churned up by the cranes and lorries which lifted the wreckage and took it away, there was no evidence that anything fatal and important had ever happened here.

What was the cause of this crash and these deaths? On the night of October 17, various theories were aired—a terrorist bomb, vandalism, some fault with the train, driver error, signal error. By the next day, however, the immediate cause was identified and publicized: a broken rail. A 100ft length of steel became the assassin, the Gavrilo Princip in the case, but, like the sluggish underlying causes and abrupt consequences of the First World War, how and why it came to break and why its shattering dislocated the life of Britain—these causes stretch back and out into the wider world of politics and history beyond Howe Dell.

We could begin in Babylonia.

2. The Permanent Way

When I was five or six years old, my elder brother took me for a walk one day down the hill through the cotton factories—this was Lancashire—to the place where a railway broke free of its tunnel. We scrambled down the embankment. My brother placed a penny on the line. Soon enough a train came past. Afterwards, smoke and steam hung lazily in the tunnel mouth. As the throb of the train receded into the distance, we stepped forward again and retrieved a wider, thinner penny with the head of King George VI flattened and disfigured by the pressure of many tons. (This may have been an offence against the realm as well as the trespass laws; it certainly caused a row when we got home.) That was the first time that I can remember coming close to a rail, bending over its burnished top surface and rusty sides as my brother (who was in the grip of the railway hobby) explained some technical terms: the wooden 'sleepers'—or 'ties' in North America—which hold the two lines of rail together (that day I remember their smell of pitch and creosote); the 'fishplates' which bolt the joins in place between each length of rail and the next; the iron 'chairs' which grip the rail and are bolted to each sleeper; last the 'ballast', the heaped chips of rock into which the sleepers are bedded.

An apparently simple technology and until the Hatfield crash I never thought about it. Who would? A steel rail to support and guide a powered wheel, a flange on the wheel to keep the wheel in place; result, traction. Writers and painters have been taken by the sheen of rails, their resolute straightness and smooth curves, since they became features of almost every landscape in the nineteenth century: rails by moonlight and in the morning sun, 'shining ribbons of steel', 'the romance of the Iron Road'. In film, they may make their most famous appearance in John Ford's *The Iron Horse*, when the labouring teams which are building America's first transcontinental railway from each coast meet in Utah and hammer the last spike home. In literature, the Australian writer Murray Bail has a fine description in his novel, *Eucalyptus*:

> The heavy rails went away parallel to the platform on the regularly spaced sleepers darkened by shadow and grease, and darkened further as they went away into the sunlight, the rails converging with a silver wobble in bushes, bend and mid-morning haze.

How rails look (Bail); how they could unify a nation (Ford); but how did they come to be? The whole assemblage—rails, sleepers, ballast—is known as 'the permanent way', so called to differentiate it from the temporary track which was laid to build the railway, its great earthworks, bridges and tunnels. The permanent way was first perfected in England, and in England still there is a learned and professional society, The Permanent Way Institution, founded by a group of railwaymen in Nottingham in 1884, to 'advance track knowledge and the spreading and exchanging of such knowledge among railwaymen throughout all railway systems at home and abroad'. Today it has 7,000 members—men mainly, though women were admitted in 1964—many of them in former colonies of the British Empire or in other parts of the world such as South America which once imported British railway technology. The institution publishes books and monographs. One of the latter, *The Evolution of Permanent Way* by Charles E. Lee, first published in 1937 and still distributed to members, addresses the question of history—originally, one suspects, to inspire the institution's membership of permanent way inspectors with an idea of vocation, of historical mission, in their long, often lonely, days and nights spent walking along miles of track. (My own father, a steam mechanic, an artisan, kept a commonplace book which contains, among the poems and pressed flowers, assorted references to George Stephenson and James Watt, so this idea of technological mission, of informing working men of their heroic antecedents, is believable to me.)

And so: Babylonia. According to Lee, a railway 'is merely a specialized form of road designed to meet limited needs'. According to Lee again, the earliest evidence of railways by this definition occurs in the Babylonian empire ruled by Belus, about 2245 BC. Around this time—not much after Middle Stone Age families were sitting around Howe Dell, chipping flints—Babylonian stonemasons were instructed to build certain imperial roads as two parallel lines of stone, 5ft (or three cubits) apart, this distance measured from the centre of each stone line, so that vehicles of the same 5ft axle width could be pulled along by mules and horses which walked down the centre of the track. This system made haulage easier, the wheels turning against smooth stone rather than rough ground, but it seems (Lee's evidence is sketchy) to have contained no means of making sure that a vehicle stayed on the track other than by the navigational instincts of its animal pullers and human drivers. Railways by their more exact definition, as prepared tracks which by their construction keep the vehicle in place and guide it independently of human or animal interference, were probably first known in Greece. When Aristophanes was alive, around 400 BC, Greek ships were pulled across the isthmus at Corinth on wheeled cradles which travelled along grooves cut into the rock. Elsewhere in Greece, images of the gods were moved to their sacrificial sites along tracks of grooved stone laid to a uniform gauge of 5ft 4in, with loops—*ektropoi*—so that vehicles might pass each other. Regular and parallel grooves, all 4ft 6in apart, can also be found in the streets of Pompeii, though whether they were ruts worn by chariot wheels or a form of guide-rails cut intentionally, Lee cannot be sure.

A prolonged and rail-less interval followed the collapse of Greek and Roman civilizations, until, around the twelfth century, German miners began to spread across central Europe in the search for exploitable seams of metal ore: iron, lead, silver, copper and gold.

Illustrated books published in Germany in the sixteenth century have lively woodcuts of bearded men in pointed woollen headwear pushing small trucks from the mine's mouth on wooden rails, while other men, similarly bearded and hatted (mines could be high in the mountains and bitterly cold), busy themselves at the rock face with hammers and picks. These illustrations, in the book *De Re Metallica* (1556) and elsewhere, are the first to depict railways—their little trucks, mines and men eventually serving as the prototypes for the industrial hi-ho situation in Disney's *Snow White* (just as the grooves cut across Corinth are the precursor of Brio's toy track). But keeping the trucks on the wooden track—making them obey, as it were, its direction—remained a large problem when both wheel and rail were flat at their point of contact, with nothing to prevent the one leaving the other. Various methods evolved. Trucks were fitted with guide pins or secondary guide wheels which ran along the rail's inner vertical surface like castors; sometimes the rails themselves were modified with U-shaped channels to hold the wheel or an extra length of wood tacked to their outer sides to form an *L* shape and give them a vertical, holding edge. It seems that nobody thought of modifying the wheel rather than the rail— perhaps because the trucks needed to be versatile and run also over rough ground—until railways spread from Europe to Britain in the seventeenth century. The breakthrough was the flange, the edge which extends beyond the wheel's running surface and prevents it going astray. The first documented railway in England (Wollaton, near Nottingham, 1603) probably had trucks with flanged wheels. Like almost every railway built in Britain over the next two centuries, the Wollaton line transported coal from a pithead; and as the coal industry grew— 210,000 tons of it dug between 1551 and 1560, 10,295,000 tons between 1781 and 1790—so railways and flanged wheels proliferated. Lines ran from collieries to ports and canals in many parts of the country; when Bonnie Prince Charlie and his Highland troops defeated the Hanoverian army at the battle of Prestonpans in 1745, they faced cannon positioned on a railway embankment built to serve a Lowland coal mine (the thought gives a jolt to romantic history). Chiefly, however, railways grew and developed on the banks of the Wear and Tyne, where the huge volumes of coal taken down steep banks to ships docked on those rivers made road transport increasingly impractical.

It was here that the railway took on its modern meaning, as locomotives replaced horses as traction, and wooden rails gave way to iron. Continental Europe, when it came to import the technology of flanged wheels and iron rails from Britain in the last quarter of the eighteenth century, knew it as the *voie anglaise* or the *englischer Schienenweg*—the English railway.

And yet, among all this modernity which placed rough and unlikely stretches of Britain at the leading edge of global change, one thing remained unconsidered and immutable: the width between the parallel rails, the gauge. In Babylonia, in Greece, at Pompeii, if not in the narrow tunnels of the European metal mines, it had always measured somewhere between 4ft and 5ft. Now, in Northumberland and Durham, so many miles and years from Babylon, it measured roughly the same. The scholarship of Lee and others suggests that this was the most efficient axle width for animal haulage; narrow it, and the load wouldn't use a horse's full pulling power; widen it, and the weight of the vehicle—the deadweight—would increase disproportionately to the load the vehicle carried. On the multiplying colliery railways of north-east England, trucks began to be exchanged between coal companies with adjacent lines and it became important to regularize their gauge. By the end of the eighteenth century many of these railways were 4ft 8in. The steam locomotive provided a massive increase in tractive effort over the horse and the gauge of a steam-powered railway could have been much wider. But, contrary to its name, the Industrial Revolution arrived by increments. The pioneering steam locomotives of the second decade of the nineteenth century were risky and not always successful experiments as horse-replacements; the gauge existed—there it was trailing down from the pit to the river over expensive bridges and piers; the easiest and cheapest thing was for steam locomotives to adopt it. In 1821, George Stephenson was appointed engineer to an ambitious new railway which would connect the north-eastern towns of Stockton and Darlington, the line which became the world's first public railway—not purely a coal owner's transport—when it was opened in 1825 to all kinds of freight from all kinds of businesses. To build the railway, to carry earth to and from its embankments and cuttings, he hired spoil trucks from the line that served a colliery at Hetton, a few miles off in County Durham. The trucks were of 4ft 8in gauge and the temporary civil-engineering line was built to fit them; Stephenson unquestioningly followed the same width for the permanent way, though sometime in the course of laying it he made a small adjustment. Previously, the right angle of the rail fitted neatly into the other right angle where the wheel joined the flange. This was too rigid for the new power and speed of steam locomotives—the constant scraping of iron against iron in this ninety-degree angle damaged both rail and wheel. Stephenson added the idea of *conicity*, curving the junction between flange and wheel and bevelling the corner of the rail to give greater play between them. Minus its sharp angles on each side, the width between the rails became 4ft 8½in.

This awkward result of conservatism, happenstance and artisanship, expressed by the metric system as 1,435mm, became one of the world's most ubiquitous measurements. When emissaries from other industrializing countries—the US, France, Prussia—came to the Stephenson factory in Newcastle, locomotives designed to that precise gauge were what they saw and sometimes purchased. A steam locomotive could still be so unreliably variable in so many ways— the difficulties and dangers of harnessing steam under pressure—that it may have been a relief to have one constant, gauge, that could be set aside as an untroubling *sine qua non*. Why worry about the rail width under the boiler, when the boiler itself might blow up? Easier, if you didn't already possess a railway, to let the locomotive determine the gauge. Later the gauge was questioned, principally by Isambard Kingdom Brunel, who built the main line from London to Bristol at 7ft ¼in—a more stable and smoother railway, with a far greater carrying capacity—and countries and colonies which first built railways after the gauge question became a public debate adopted various widths: wider in Ireland, Russia and India, narrower in some parts of Australia and Africa. But Stephenson's gauge became the standard where it mattered, at the centre and not the periphery of the industrial world in the first half of the nineteenth century, and in these places Brunel lost his cause.

Of the 750,000 route miles of railway which exist in the world today, sixty per cent measure 4ft 8½in from rail to rail. Across and under the Rockies, the Alps, and the Thames and the Hudson, past the cherry slopes of Mount Fujiyama, spreading into webs of freight yards, converging at junctions; shining and exact parallels, the reasons for their particular exactness lost to the mainstream of history. Trains followed this gauge to the battlefields of the American Civil War and the Somme, into the Vatican City, to the tragic little terminus under the gate at Auschwitz. On this gauge, Buster Keaton outwitted the Union army. Across it, many silent heroines were tied. Riding above it, Cary Grant kissed Eva Marie Saint and remarked: 'The train's a little unsteady' (and in their bedroom on the Twentieth Century Limited, Eva Marie Saint replied: 'Who isn't?').

And of course on October 17 last year it was also the gauge that carried the 12.10 north from London, with 170 passengers including four men of middle age named Alcorn, Arthur, Monkhouse and Gray. Five minutes out of King's Cross, somewhere between Finsbury Park and Hornsey if my frequent experience is any guide, an announcement was made from the buffet car. It was open and selling 'traditional and gourmet sandwiches, hot toasties, pastries, and hot and cold drinks'.

The four men rose and swayed down the train to coach G. The Alexandra Palace went by on its green hill. The train accelerated and bore on through the tunnels and stations of the north London suburbs: New Southgate, Oakleigh Park, New Barnet, Potters Bar. The names of the stations became too blurred by speed to read, the tunnels no more than a momentary darkness and a change of noise and pressure that shuddered the carriage windows.

Thirteen miles out: the first countryside—cows, woods, what might still be a farmhouse. A mobile phone or two rang out its simple tune: *Für Elise*, 'British Grenadiers'. The four men were probably in the buffet car by now. Small bottles of Merlot Cabernet jiggled in a glass cabinet. Steam hissed from the tea and coffee machine. Hot bread filled with bubbling cheese popped from the toaster.

Fourteen miles out, Brookmans Park. A mile and thirty seconds later, Welham Green. Some flat modern factories and warehouses appeared on the left with large and legible signs: SOUNDCRAFT, TESCO, FALCON FOR GAMES, PUZZLES AND PLAYING CARDS, MITSUBISHI. If any of the four men looked out of the window at this point, Mitsubishi would be the last word he ever read.

3. The trouble with rails

The first rails to be made completely of metal came out of the Dowlais ironworks in South Wales in 1791. They were cast iron, much more durable than wood but also brittle; they broke. The great quest in the 210-year history of rails since then has been *to find a rail that will not break*—or not at least inside the parameters of the load it is expected to carry within its allotted lifespan. The answer, for a time, was wrought or malleable iron—iron beaten with hammers or pressed through rollers, rather than poured into casts to cool and harden. Wrought iron was more fibrous, many of the impurities had been beaten out of it; it had a greater tensile strength. In 1820, John Birkinshaw of the Bedlington Ironworks in Northumberland patented 'An Improvement in the Construction of Malleable Iron Rails...whereby the Expence of Repairs of broken rails [is] saved'. Each of Birkinshaw's rails had been squeezed six times between the cylinders of his rolling mill and emerged at unprecedented lengths of up to 18ft—'to reduce the shocks or jolts to which the carriages are subject from passing over the joints (very much to the injury of the machinery)'. Stephenson used Birkinshaw rails for the Stockton and Darlington and again later on the world's first passenger railway, the Liverpool and Manchester, where they were laid in 15ft lengths weighing 35lb a yard. They also broke. By 1832, only two years after the railway opened, it was noticed that fragments of iron littered the track. New rails were ordered at steadily increasing weights, first 50lb a yard, then 60lb, then 75lb. By 1839, every one of the line's original rails had been replaced.

Eleven years later, when the Great Northern Railway opened its main line between London and Peterborough via Hatfield, the pattern was repeated. The trains curved past Howe Dell on 18ft lengths of wrought iron rail which weighed 72lb to the yard. They too soon began to chip and fragment under the weight of heavy coal traffic. A few miles south, at Barnet, it was judged that the life of a rail was no more than three and a half years. The Great Northern ordered new wrought iron rails and upped their weight by 10lb a yard. By 1865, the entire line had been re-railed. But the new rails proved only slightly more reliable than the old. Trains ran at increasing frequency, load and speed, and the manufacture of good wrought iron depended too much on human skill, which varied from shift to shift and works to works.

Railways began to experiment with steel—a strong, supple iron alloy formed by blasting air through iron during the smelting process to remove the carbon content, the invention patented by Sir Henry Bessemer in 1855. Steel rails were a third more expensive, but trials showed that they lasted four to six times longer than wrought iron. By the 1880s almost every main line in England, including the Great Northern's, had been relaid in steel, but that too had problems. Steel could last for years, shining brightly in the signal lights, apparently perfect, and then suddenly it would snap. Accidents were rare from this cause, but two passengers died at St Neots, thirty-five miles north of Hatfield, when broken steel rails threw a train off the line in 1895. In 1899, members of the Institution of Civil Engineers in London worried about the 'capricious' nature of steel rails and their 'remarkable vagaries'. British engineers studied the new science of metal fatigue, mainly the work of the German metallurgist, August Wohler (an early example of what became a reverse flow of railway know-how, as Britain imported new knowledge and techniques from Europe and the US). Rails became heavier still; on the line past Howe Dell they weighed 100lb a yard by 1914, 109lb by 1950. Their shape changed. In the middle nineteenth century, rails had been made with the head (the top) the same as the foot (the bottom), to give two potential running surfaces, so that after one was worn out the rail could be turned upside down, doubling its life. The idea didn't work—the base-plates left dents in the bottom surface—but the shape was retained for a hundred years. They were known as 'bullheads', and their replacements in the 1950s as 'flatbottoms'—the usual shape in Europe and North America. The noise made by the combination of track and train began to change around the same time. The wheels no longer ran clackety-clack over the joins ('What's the train saying?' our fathers would say. '*Peas-and-beans, peas-and-beans, peas-and-beans*? Or is it *fish-and-chips, fish-and-chips, fish-and-chips*? What's for tea?') British engineers followed European practice and welded the lengths of rail together. The tiny gap between each rail length disappeared. Concrete sleepers replaced wood, and the rails were bolted or spiked directly to them—no intervening 'chairs'—as the US had done from the beginning. In combination, these changes made the rails more durable and saved money on repairs. When trains ran over continuously welded track the cost of their tractive energy was cut by five per cent, by the single act of removing the tiny gap or the infinitesimal difference in position between one rail and the next; the price of peas-and-beans.

Then, in 1967, forty-nine passengers died when a train derailed on unwelded track at Hither Green in south London. The cause was a rail which had fractured at its weakest point, the bolt-holes at the join. Rails thereafter were made to a new specification, with a thicker 'web'—the spine which joins railhead to railfoot—and a new weight of 113lb.

This became the standard British rail, specification BS11–113A. In 1995, as part of regular repair and maintenance work, new rails of this kind were laid at Howe Dell. Like most rails in Britain, they were made by British Steel (now part of an Anglo-Dutch company, Corus) at its plant in Workington, Cumbria. They weren't quite standard. When rails are expected to carry an extra stress, they are especially hardened at the factory by quenching them with water as soon as they leave the rollers, a process called 'mill heat treatment'. These were mill heat treated (MHT) rails; they were to be laid on the curve. And curves bring their own problems.

4. The trouble with curves

Engineering is often easier to depict than to describe. One striking thing about engineers—apart from their disenchantment with the managerial class set above them and the trivialized culture which neglects them—is how often they want to draw things; words not being up to the work of describing the technical reality. During the research for this piece, I was handed several instant drawings. 'Give us a pen,' engineers would say, 'Look, it works like this.'

In a phenomenon known as 'the dynamics of the wheel/rail interface', drawing is especially useful. One day in November I took the train from London to Peterborough—a very slow train which moved gingerly over the crash site—to meet a young engineer, Philip Haigh, who writes for the specialist magazine, *Rail*. 'Give us a pen,' he said at one point, and then: 'Do you have a 5p piece?' He drew round the circumference of the coin to produce a circle with a diameter of about ³⁄₄in or 2cm. That was the size of the contact area between a wheel and a rail when train and track were in perfect equilibrium. Perfection requires the straightest rail and the truest wheel; but if these ideal conditions were met, Haigh said, then only a ³⁄₄in strip would wear along the rail top (which is 2³⁄₄in wide). In an electric locomotive, 100 tons of vehicle and machinery could be shared among eight wheels and eight of these 5p contact spots. Each 5p would support a weight of 12.5 tons. Given a powerful engine, the friction caused by turning all eight wheels against two rails would easily haul a train of 1,000 tons at 115 miles an hour.

And when the train reaches a curve? 'The contact spot shifts for both wheel and rail,' Haigh said. What happens is this: the wheels are asked to obey a new direction by the rail. That instruction, combined with centrifugal force, pushes the wheel against the rail on the outside of a curve. The shoulder between flange and wheel hits the corner of the rail. At low speed, that hardly matters, the train will scrape round. At high speed, say 125 mph, the train needs some corrective to try to restore its equilibrium. Therefore the track is 'canted'—tilted like the racing track in a velodrome, with the outside rail the higher of the two. But different kinds of train travel at different speeds and would need different levels of cant if their equilibrium was always to be perfect. Engineers reach a compromise: a cant that will work at different speeds, though not perfectly for all of them. The difference between the ideal cant for a high-speed train and the most practical cant for all trains is known as 'cant deficiency'. At high speed, the wheels still shift position and put an extra stress on the higher rail, attacking its inner corner, the corner from which the gauge is measured: the gauge corner.

Rails are made to take pressure from the top. Exposed to this different, sideways pressure from, say sixty fast trains a day, seven days a week, they can begin to crack: gauge corner cracking. Mill heat treatment prevents that; or does it? The answer seems to be yes and no. It may modify a rail's first inclination to crack, but once a crack has started, a softer rail may be the better option. Softer rails wear faster, perhaps faster than cracks can grow; a crack can be worn away before it has the chance to dive down into the heart of the rail. In Haigh's word, a softer rail can be 'self-correcting'. (Metallurgists

THE HATFIELD CRASH

1. The cause: gauge corner cracking

The normal contact area between wheel and rail is on the rail top. When the wheels of trains travelling at high speed hit a curve, sideways thrust creates a different area of contact by pushing the wheel's flange against the rail's inner or 'gauge' corner. The stress in the steel, repeated hundreds of times a week, can cause tiny cracks.

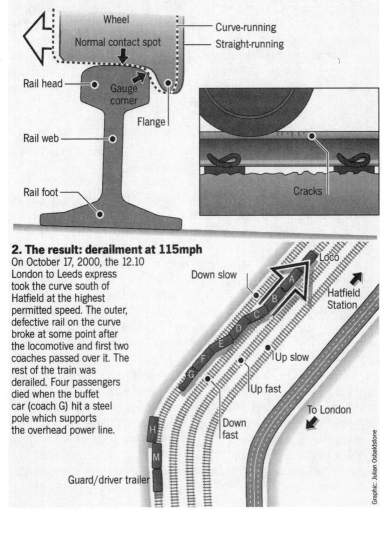

Wheel

Normal contact spot

Curve-running

Straight-running

Rail head

Gauge corner

Flange

Rail web

Rail foot

Cracks

2. The result: derailment at 115mph

On October 17, 2000, the 12.10 London to Leeds express took the curve south of Hatfield at the highest permitted speed. The outer, defective rail on the curve broke at some point after the locomotive and first two coaches passed over it. The rest of the train was derailed. Four passengers died when the buffet car (coach G) hit a steel pole which supports the overhead power line.

Loco

Down slow

Hatfield Station

A

B

C

D

E

F

Up slow

G

Up fast

To London

H

Down fast

M

Guard/driver trailer

Graphic: Julian Osbaldstone

and engineers debate this. However, the rails which replaced those destroyed in the crash at Howe Dell were not heat-treated, and none of them have been laid since.)

Curves are by no means the only cause of damaged rails. The steel may contain flaws, little voids (*tache ovales*) which are difficult and sometimes impossible to detect by the human eye. Wheels which are out of shape and not perfectly circular (*wheel flats*) can batter and dent the rail—like gauge corner cracking this comes under the general heading of *rolling contact fatigue*. The ground beneath can subside by an inch and twist the rail. The railhead can flake (*spalling*). The more I read about the subject (example *Residual Stress in Rails*, by Orringer, Orkisz and Swiderski, Kluwer Academic Publishers, volume one, 1992—but let's not go there), the more engineers I talked to, the more I saw rails in a new light; not as simple and indestructible—the Iron Road—but as complicated and vulnerable. Railway engineers have always seen them in this way, as a technology that requires constant vigilance.

At a railway engineering exhibition in Birmingham, I met a retired permanent way engineer, Bill Armstrong, who spoke about the track as 'a living thing'. Ballast could 'develop a memory'; rails always wanted 'to go back to where they lived before'. This was in the context of track-relaying, the dangers of putting new line over old ballast furrowed by sleepers or old rails into new positions on a curve, where they would show signs of wanting to resume their original shape and need to be beaten back, with hammers. Rails were always shifting, settling, creeping this way or that. As the chief permanent way engineer for a large part of Yorkshire, in the old coal district between Doncaster and Leeds, he'd been required to walk every mile of his track twice a year; the main line and three tributary passenger branches, several colliery lines, a large freight yard—many dozens of miles on foot, twice a year, peering at the rails. The inspectors under him walked every mile of track under their care at least once a month; in turn, the sub-inspectors under them walked it at least once a fortnight. Then there were the permanent way gangers—labourers—who would also walk their particular stretch. In this way, every mile of line was patrolled not less than twice a week. Passenger lines were inspected no fewer than three times, usually on Mondays, Wednesdays and Fridays. 'We had a saying,' Armstrong said. 'The uninspected inevitably deteriorates.'

We were talking inside one of the bleak halls of Birmingham's National Exhibition Centre. The Hatfield crash had cast a gloom over this year's trade fair. At a couple of seminars in side rooms I'd heard speakers despair of the national culture: 'a dearth of engineers...a basic lack of engineering competence which is a problem across the board in the industry...not enough people who understand how the infrastructure works or behaves'. In the hall, videos at several stands showed pieces of machinery and stressed that 'safety is our number one priority'. The words had become the new railway mantra.

Armstrong, who was manning a stall for the Permanent Way Institution, said: 'How many folk in this country, even the ones who're interested in railways, know what happens below the wheel? With them, it's always the wheel upwards, the stuff on top, never below the wheel. Below the wheel matters. You know the trouble with England? We've never had the guts to rip things down and start again. It's all make do and mend.' He had an analogy. 'It's like having a wife who keeps asking you to paint the front door when the more important job is to get the damp seen to in the cellar.'

He spoke about an everyday garden nuisance, one apparently far removed from the dynamics of the wheel–rail interface: the weed. 'In the old days you'd never see a weed on the line. That was when you had six chaps working from the same hut, looking after their bit of track. Weeds are unsightly, they're evidence of neglect, they clog the drainage in the ballast, the ballast becomes uneven, the tracks sink or twist. It's like a house, the permanent way. You get your foundations right, you get your drainage right, and you build up from there.'

And now? 'The days of a line being patrolled by a man every day have gone. But it's worse than that. Not only have the maintenance structures disappeared, but the knowledge of what the structures *did* has disappeared.'

The great change happened in the middle years of the 1990s, its centrepiece the Railways Act which was passed by the Conservative government in 1993. Seven years later, at 12.23 p.m. last October 17, the 12.10 to Leeds came off the tracks. The two events are connected.

There was a fracture on the outer high rail at the Hatfield curve.

The locomotive and the train's first two coaches passed over it safely, but the shock and pressure ran through the rail like a lightning bolt. The pressure found other cracks; there were cracks everywhere. Instantly, more than a 100 ft of rail shattered into 300 pieces. The other eight vehicles came off the track. Passengers fell over each other, necks hit the backs of seats. Scalding water exploded in the buffet car. Apart from the dead—Alcorn, Arthur, Monkhouse and Gray—two buffet attendants and two other passengers were seriously injured, another sixty-six passengers slightly so.

Ambulances came. Howe Dell flickered with flashing lights and the arcing sparks of acetylene torches. By 2.30 p.m., the first officers had arrived from government agencies: the Health and Safety Executive, its quaintly named sub division Her Majesty's Railway Inspectorate, and the British Transport Police. For the next four days they bent among the ballast and the grass and picked up pieces of steel. Eventually they reconstructed the assassin, the rail, and named the assassin's weapon, gauge corner cracking. A remote technical term entered the common language. But if rail and cracks were Gavrilo Princip and his pistol, who was the Kaiser in the case? The truth is that there were several kaisers—stubborn men in love with a political idea that they imagined would fulfil the national destiny. One of them lived just down the track at Huntingdon: the former prime minister, John Major.

5. Trainspotting

Railways as an interest, a hobby like philately or butterfly collecting, began in the late nineteenth century, when English gentlemen with time on their hands (lawyers, vicars) started to see steam locomotives as fascinating objects in themselves rather than purely as the source of the most convenient means of transport. They would pursue rare types, exchange notes, lug plate cameras and tripods to the tops of cuttings, take photographs of expresses (always from a distance and head on, to avoid too much blurring). By 1897 two magazines catered for these hobbyists. Two years later they had a club, the Railway Club, with armchaired rooms in London.

What would one of these trainspotters have seen at Howe Dell? The Great Northern Railway had been built to shorten the distance from London to Yorkshire, to compete against a longer and slower route, and in the closing decades of the nineteenth century it had a service of swift and regular trains which was said to be unrivalled in the world. In 1889, the Shah of Persia came down the 185 miles from Leeds to London in three hours forty-two minutes, and that included a fifteen-minute stop for lunch at Grantham (where Mrs Margaret, now Baroness, Thatcher's grandfather was a station cloakroom attendant). An enthusiast leaning on the fence at Howe Dell would have seen smart little green locomotives and teak-brown carriages rushing north at a mile a minute and long coal trains winding slowly south from the northern coalfields to the London depots. Gleaming paintwork and brass, the oil lamp of a signal flickering red though the smoke; superficially, the golden age of Britain's railways. Less golden, however, to the railway shareholder. Britain had a denser network of railways than any other country; travellers from London to Manchester, for example, could choose between four different routes owned by four different companies. Such extreme competition cut into profits. The average return on railway shares between 1850 and 1875 was a modest 3.65 per cent. The most profitable lines were often small local monopolies whose main business was the transport of minerals. Many companies made no money at all. Public ownership was considered by governments as early as the First World War, but in 1923 a different solution was chosen. Britain's 120 railway companies were amalgamated into four large groups, with the government intending that each of them would become a profitable regional monopoly. The Great Northern became part of the London and North Eastern Railway, the LNER. It built more powerful locomotives and painted them a lighter green; its expresses to the north got faster; in 1938, it claimed the world record speed for a steam locomotive, 126 mph, which has never been bettered. But profit was still difficult because by now the competition wasn't from rival railway companies but from a new means of transport: roads, cars, coaches, lorries. In the years leading up to the Second World War, the LNER paid its shareholders no dividends at all. In 1946, it managed 0.41 per cent. For a Labour government committed to the post-war reconstruction of Britain's damaged infrastructure, there could be only one solution. In 1948, as part of a pattern common throughout Europe, the railways of Britain were taken into public ownership and became British Railways, later British Rail. Initial public investment halted their decline, but that proved temporary. Roads increasingly drew away their freight and passengers and their subsidy became unpopular in the Treasury. Golden Ageism was never far from the surface of post-war Britain and the feeling grew, especially among Conservative politicians and commentators, that things had been better arranged in the days of gleaming paintwork and brass, when porters tipped their caps when you slipped them sixpence. Over the next thirty years, the railways were 'rationalized'—lines closed, staff cut—until by the 1980s they were the most cost-effective and had the lowest level of government subsidy of any country in western Europe (still unchanged in 1996, when the figures for planned investment over the following four years, per head of population, were: France, £21; Switzerland, £40; Italy, £33; Britain, £9). There was by this time no political belief in them. Mrs Thatcher, the railwayman's granddaughter, made a point of never travelling by train and spoke of 'the great car economy'. Two other phrases began to be applied to railways in her era, 'value engineering' and 'the management of decline'. In the late 1980s, when the East Coast Main Line through Hatfield was electrified, first to Leeds and than all the way to Edinburgh, it was said to be the cheapest such scheme in Europe, where countries such as France and Italy copied the Japanese model and built, at great expense, new straight railways dedicated to high-speed trains, with their rails embedded in continuous concrete. In France, the permitted top speed was 300 kilometres per hour; in Germany, 280 kph; in Italy, 250 kph; in Britain, 200 kph (125 mph). In Britain, the new trains through Hatfield were built at a cost of 23,100 US dollars per seat. In Europe, nothing similar was achieved for under 35,885 US dollars per seat (the new trains built for the Channel Tunnel, London to Paris, cost almost 50,000 US dollars per seat). In Britain, the overhead power lines would blow down in high winds. Their suspension support was not robust.

Within railways, among railway people, there came an important cultural shift. The future of subsidies was uncertain, 'profit-centres' had been created. In this climate, operators—the executives who timetabled and managed the trains—became more important than engineers. In the words of Michael Casebourne, the chief executive of the Institution of Civil Engineers: 'The railways had a tremendous number of engineers, sometimes leading authorities in rail engineering worldwide or in touch with other people who were. They were authoritarian, highly responsible and very good at what they did, and they ran the railway from a protective point of view. An awful lot of what they did—resignalling and track work—interrupted the running of the trains. Consequently, they got a very bad name with the operators and just before privatization, the balance changed—it became an operators' rather than an engineers' railway.'

Privatization, Casebourne added, 'had the effect of reinforcing many of these views'.

6. Ideology

During successive Conservative governments between 1979 and 1997 more than two thirds of Britain's state-owned industry was sold to the private sector, transferring about a million jobs and raising £65bn for the Treasury. Mrs Thatcher wanted to 'roll back the frontiers of the state'; a wider spread of shareholders would create 'popular capitalism', and by exposing state industries to market forces they would become more efficient and offer cheaper goods or a better service to the consumer. The cash raised meant that the government could avoid the more electorally dangerous alternatives of raising taxes or cutting public expenditure. Harold Macmillan, a former and more patrician Conservative prime minister, called it 'selling the family silver'.

The results were uneven. Several public utilities—the gas, water and telecommunications industries—were sold off en bloc to become private monopolies, no more responsive to the market or the consumer than when they were owned by the state. There was public disenchantment. Advocates of privatization blamed lack of competition, which in their view was the key element in raising efficiency. When the turn came for the electricity industry to be privatized, the government broke it down into more than a dozen generating and distribution companies. This seemed to work; competition between them produced efficiency—lower costs. The promotion of competition became a key element in future privatization schemes, and the electricity industry a model for the railways.

By several accounts, Mrs Thatcher had little personal enthusiasm for privatizing British Rail, realizing (perhaps) that if it went wrong she risked the Conservative vote in the London commuter belt. Unlike the electricity industry, trains—more important, fares—depended on government subsidy that was running close to £1bn a year. But two of her successive Ministers for Transport, Paul Channon and Cecil Parkinson, eventually persuaded her to include it in the Conservative agenda and in 1990 Parkinson announced to Parliament that the government was 'determined to privatize British Rail'.

Nobody had any clear idea of how, or at least no single clear idea that had unanimous appeal to Conservative think tanks, Cabinet ministers, transport economists, civil servants and British Rail itself. Ideas varied. One obvious solution was to break British Rail into several regional monopolies in a new version of the railway companies which existed between 1923 and 1948. Mrs Thatcher's successor, the English nostalgist, John Major, seemed for a time to favour that and the Conservative manifesto for the 1992 general election included the hope that the new railways would 'reflect regional and local identity [and] recapture the spirit of the old regional companies'. But the trouble with this scenario of gleaming paint and polite porters—Major himself mentioned the Great Western Railway's brown and cream carriages—was that it introduced very little in the way of a new competitive element (ignoring the fact that competition against rival forms of transport, roads and airlines, already existed). A structure needed to be found which would provide *competition within the railway itself*—and it needed to be found quickly. Major won the 1992 election with his railway privatization scheme little more than a blank piece of paper (in the later words of his new Transport Minister, John MacGregor); the legislation would need to be passed and the privatization successfully implemented by the time the next election was due in 1997. There was very little left to privatize. Major, who was aware of his mild public image, needed a privatization of his own to demonstrate his radical credentials as Mrs Thatcher's heir.

Horizontal separation—the railways as regional monopolies—kept trains, stations, track, signalling and general infrastructure under one ownership, the way they had always been. Vertical separation was a more radical solution. It would separate trains from rails. The owner of the rails would charge the owners of the trains for access to them, on the same principle as a toll road. Different train owners could compete for passengers and freight on the same stretch of track. The idea found favour in Major's old department, the Treasury, and though the object of it has never been achieved (very few train companies compete for the same traffic over the same line), the competitive principle behind it was used to fragment Britain's railways into more than a hundred separate businesses, about the same number that had been amalgamated in 1923.

When the plan was published in a White Paper in 1992, it aroused considerable hostility. Opinion polls showed that a large majority of the public was against it, the Labour Party in opposition fought it, and even the Conservative press was sceptical. The Conservative Party itself was divided. A Conservative Member of Parliament, the late Robert Adley, interrogated ministers from his position as the chairman of Parliament's Transport Select Committee, and concluded that 'it seems to me that none of them, quite frankly, have a clue about how all this is going to be worked out'. Of all privatization schemes, the railways soon became the most disliked, with few supporters outside the government and the financiers and commercial lawyers of the City of London who stood to gain. One Transport Minister succeeded another—a total of six in seven years, each as uncertain as his predecessor—but Major and his government stubbornly pressed ahead with the legislation, and on April 1, 1994, the Railways Act came into effect. British Rail's assets could now be sold off, under a plan that had six broad elements and a flurry of acronyms.

The passenger trains were to be run by about twenty Train Operating Companies (TOCS) on franchises which ran from between seven and fifteen years.

The trains would be owned by three Rolling Stock Companies (ROSCOS) which would lease them to the TOCS.

The railway signalling, the permanent way, bridges, tunnels and some of the larger stations would be owned by one large infrastructure company, Railtrack.

Railtrack would contract out the maintenance and renewal of the infrastructure by competitive tender to civil engineering companies (which had bought British Rail's engineering assets). They in turn might put out the work to subcontractors.

A new independent body, the Office of the Rail Regulator (ORR), would set the amount that Railtrack was allowed to charge the TOCS—the track access charges—and in general promote competition, efficiency and safety inside Railtrack, to the eventual benefit of passengers.

Another new body, the Office of Passenger Rail Franchising (OPRAF) would decide which TOC got which franchise, adjudicate the level of public subsidy required by the TOC (this was a privatization that actually increased public subsidy rather than ending or shrinking it), and reward or penalize train operating performance through a system of bonuses and penalties. Later, under the Labour Government, OPRAF became the Strategic Rail Authority, the SRA.

Six years later, it was hard to find anyone who would defend this structure, outside the Labour Government. A paradox. In opposition the Labour Party was committed to dismantling privatization and restoring a 'publicly-owned, public-accountable railway'. On March 23, 1995, the party's new leader, Tony Blair, described the privatization plan as 'absurd'. He said: 'They [the Conservatives] want to replace a comprehensive, coordinated national railway network with a hotchpotch of private companies linked together by a gigantic bureaucratic paperchase of contracts—overseen of course by a clutch of quangos [quasi-autonomous non-governmental organizations, then a favourite opposition target]. As the public learn more about the chaos and cost, their anger at this folly will grow.' The prediction came true in every respect. But as the 1997 election came closer, the party changed its stance. Under the influence of Gordon Brown, later the head of the Treasury as Chancellor of the Exchequer, no such commitment was included in the manifesto. Labour was anxious to be seen as 'prudent'; taking back the railways, or even just Railtrack, into public ownership would cost too much. In any case, as Brown told a colleague, 'privatization will make the Tories unpopular and save us from having to do it'. In government, Prime Minister Blair told an early Cabinet meeting that railways were 'not a priority'.

British Rail was sold for a total of £5bn. Government subsidies to the railway industry for the three years 1997–2000 come to roughly the same amount. The infrastructure went to Railtrack for £1.93bn. Its market value by 2000 was just under three times as much. Thanks to stubborn political pressure, emanating from a prime minister who feared to be seen as weak, the railways had been sold off hastily, cheaply and carelessly, often to owners for whom 'the wheel/rail interface' was a term of management rather than science (if it meant anything to them at all). Of Railtrack's thirteen board members, only two had railway experience and only one was an engineer. From 1997 they were led by a chief executive, Gerald Corbett, who had previously worked as the finance director for the hotels and leisure group, Grand Metropolitan. Corbett, who bears a striking resemblance to the English character actor, Timothy West, became a familiar figure on television after the crash at Ladbroke Grove in 1999 and again after Hatfield. He was sincere and he was sorry, so much so that, after Hatfield, Railtrack adopted a new slogan, SORRY IS NOT ENOUGH, and pasted it to the windows of its London headquarters and on poster sites by the side of the track. No irony seemed intended personally against the chief executive; the poster went on to say that Railtrack was working hard to give Britain a first-class railway system. At Victoria station, some delayed passenger had seen a nice anagram. The graffiti on the poster read LIARTRACK.

In other ways Corbett's regime at Railtrack could be seen as a success. The company made a profit, its share price rose steeply and the shares paid growing dividends (26.9p per share for the financial year 1999–2000, increased by five per cent after the Hatfield crash to keep the confidence of shareholders). Property was one source of profit. In the four years since Railtrack's flotation in 1996, the rent and sale of some of the buildings and land which the company had so cheaply acquired raised more than £500m. In 1999–2000, about a quarter of total profit came from property sales alone. Railtrack's chief income, however, came from the track access charges paid by the train operators—charges which were fixed in the public interest at retail price inflation minus two per cent by the Rail Regulator. If the train operators ran more trains, the charges could be adjusted upwards very slightly; in 1995 nobody, including the Rail Regulator, expected more trains. Five years later, the figure for passenger mileage had grown by thirty per cent and for freight by forty per cent as Britain came out of economic recession, motorways got clogged and train operators adopted aggressive marketing. More people were using the railways than at any time since 1946. The rails they used took more wear, but only a fraction of the increased revenue from passengers was passed on to Railtrack. Worse, more trains meant more track congestion and more delays. The Rail Regulator had set targets for punctuality expressed in percentage points. Every percentage point missed and judged to be Railtrack's fault led to a fine of £1m. In 2000, Railtrack faced a fine of £10m.

So how to make a profit from the infrastructure itself, or at least keep the cost of maintaining it down? The answer lay in scrutinizing the fine print of contractual obligation and putting more work out to tender, 'efficiency savings' which the Rail Regulator himself was keen on. In the aftermath of three rail disasters, this was said to be 'putting profit before safety'. On the trackside, it was rarely as simple as that.

At Hatfield, the technology of track and trains was now split among at least five different managements. Two companies ran the passenger trains, West Anglia Great Northern (WAGN) to the suburbs and Cambridge, the Great North Eastern Railway (GNER) to Leeds, Newcastle and Scotland, with trains leased from a separate rolling-stock company. Railtrack ran the signalling and owned the line. The line was maintained and repaired by the civil engineers, Balfour Beatty, under contract to Railtrack. Another civil engineering firm, Jarvis, had the contract for track replacement.

The 12.10 GNER express to Leeds was ultimately owned by a bank (the Hong Kong and Shanghai), leased by a Bermuda-registered shipping company (GNER is a subsidiary of Sea Containers), and given its green light by a Railtrack signaller. None of them was at fault. The trouble was the rail.

7. Workers

My route to work in London every morning takes me over a railway bridge. A traveller on the top deck of a bus at this point can see a junction and a single line curving off into a tunnel. Once there were two lines; once the curve was smooth. Sometime in the early 1990s, however, I noticed that one of the lines had been taken up and that the curve was really a series of angled straight rails. Bill Armstrong, the old permanent way man, described this to me as 'a threepenny-bit curve', after the old British dodecagonal coin. The rails had probably been used elsewhere, or turned around at the same site, and wanted to assume their previous form, 'to go back,' as he said, 'to where they lived before'. Also, around the same time, I began to notice weeds here and on other lines; weeds that grew on the ballast sometimes to the size of small shrubs. Even the busy track outside Waterloo terminus had them, with their suggestion of abandoned railways in the Argentinian pampas. I imagined that railways were obeying a new ecological stricture to ban herbicide. The cause was more straightforward.

Between 1992 and 1997, the number of people employed on Britain's railways fell from 159,000 to 92,000 at a time when the number of trains increased. Within these totals, the numbers of workers permanently employed to maintain and renew the infrastructure fell from 31,000 to between 15,000 and 19,000. In a rare piece of enquiring journalism on the subject, the *Guardian*'s labour correspondent, Keith Harper, interviewed some permanent way workers in March, 1998. They were men aged between forty-five and fifty, 'the rump of what is left of British Rail's skilled workforce,' as Harper described them, and they spoke scathingly of the methods of their new employers, the private contractors who worked for Railtrack. Harper kept them anonymous; speaking to the press—'whistle-blowing'—is now usually a breach of contract. One worker said:

> At least fifty per cent of the track is on its last legs. If it's not broken rails, it's broken components. If the public knew the full picture, it would be horrified. There are accidents waiting to happen and loads of speed restrictions. Some cowboy [casual worker] the other day forgot to put up a 20 mph speed restriction on a 70 mph route. How there wasn't an accident I'll never know.

Another said:

> Railtrack is really responsible for seeing that the work gets done properly, but my work has never been checked by Railtrack and, in my time, I have worked on some extremely dodgy jobs that

require proper inspection. It is up to the maintenance companies to do it, but they often sub-contract work to many fly-by-night operators. They bring in gangs of casuals in taxis and pay them eighty pounds in hard cash for a shift.

A third said:

Railtrack is a joke. It is totally reliant on the maintenance companies and does not know what is going on. Railtrack is so pious. It wrings its hands and says that safety is paramount, yet it gets really nasty if we cannot do a job on time, usually because the time we get to do it is impossible.

In November last year, attending a session of the government inquiry into the Ladbroke Grove rail crash, which is chaired by Lord Cullen, I heard the same situation on the track described in a more academic way. Professor Christopher Baldry, head of the Department of Management and Organization at Stirling University, was giving evidence about safety practices among permanent way workers, based on recent research. He used the phrase 'work intensification'.

Counsel: 'What is that?'
Baldry: 'Well, work intensification...can either be the same number of people producing more over a given time period, the same number of people producing the same volume over a shorter time period or a smaller number of people producing a given volume, if technology and other factors are held constant.'
Counsel: 'When you look at the work intensification and the figures which support that, the conclusion which you reach is that there is a worsening safety record and a worsening trend in employee safety in the [railway] industry?'
Baldry: 'Yes, this seemed to us [himself and his fellow researcher] to be what was indicated by the figures. Basically we took the figures for the amount of traffic in rail miles, an index of workload, we looked at the decline in direct employees of both Railtrack and the major contractors, although...this does not include subcontractors which is one of the defects of the official figures, but certainly the continuing downward trend in employment and the

continuing upward trend in the amount of traffic carried, I think you can take as an index of work intensification: a smaller number of people are coping with a larger volume of traffic in the network.'

How had this happened? Baldry:

If you are bidding for a contract on what is essentially a labour-intensive process, the only way or one of the major ways you are more likely to win the contract is through offering to do it with reduced labour costs, that is either to do the work with a smaller number of people or in a shorter timeframe.

Baldry went on to describe the long and unregulated hours that could be worked under the negligent eye of a subcontractor, the lack of communication between train crews, signallers and permanent way men—now all employed by different companies and often new to their jobs—and the rivalry between different contractors or subcontractors.

We were given on several occasions evidence that if, for example track workers from Scotland had been sent down to York to work on a bit of track that was unfamiliar to them, they find themselves working with other employees of a different contractor. Their instinct is to ask local people about the nature of the track. The local people may have been told by their employer 'Don't talk to these persons because they are employed by the opposition.' In other words, there are actual obstacles put in the way of site knowledge and hazards knowledge. We encountered that in several locations.

Familiarity with the track had gone, old patterns of trust had been broken; the price of the competitive spirit. There could be so many different companies employed on the same stretch of line, Baldry said, that it would take 'a very brave person' to halt the work because of a potential hazard. He had heard reports that safety representatives had been threatened with physical violence when they suggested that work should stop. 'It takes quite a brave individual to say stop the work because of the financial penalties that then rebound back up the system if the work in progress runs over time.'

The system that Baldry mentioned was designed by commercial lawyers, in the legal belief that punishment works, and it involves confusing flows of money and paperwork between many 'interfaces'— in the managerial sense—between groups which have different and sometimes conflicting financial interests. When a contracting firm repairs a track, it 'takes possession' of it. Trains are stopped for the duration of these 'track possessions' and this may in itself cost Railtrack money, if it cannot meet its obligations to the train operating companies and their trains are cancelled or delayed. If a track possession overruns its scheduled time, however, the penalties are fiercer. Track work usually takes place at the weekend—but say something unexpected occurs or the contractor has underestimated the time the repairs will take and the track possession runs into Monday morning? There is a schedule with tariffs. Rates differ. A delay to a train in the London morning rush hour, for example, can cost Railtrack £200 a minute at Waterloo and £147 a minute at Euston. One delayed train can cause other delayed trains for hundreds of miles down the track, with Railtrack compensating their operators for each. A bill of £250,000 is quite easy to run up. Railtrack, therefore, can penalize the contractor, gathering in money with one hand as it pays out with the other. Whatever emotion this system appeals to—fear, greed, blame, retribution—it is unlikely to inspire either trust or careful workmanship. (Imagine the following sequence of events. A man working for a contractor on the line notices that a rail has some cracks. He consults his supervisor. His supervisor consults Railtrack. How long will the rail last? A track possession will delay trains and cost money. Can a repair be done quickly? Might it be postponed? Need it be done at all? Doesn't it suit the contractor to have the rail replaced at Railtrack's cost, via another contractor? A new rail will cost the maintenance contractor less to maintain. That, a suspicious Railtrack official might think, might lead the contractor to overestimate the damage. Which person, at what rank, will decide what must be done?)

In July 1999, the government appointed a new Rail Regulator, Tom Winsor, himself a commercial lawyer. Winsor was determined to be tough. He wanted the trains to run to time. For him, Railtrack was 'a supplier not a dictator…it is not the king, that position belongs to the customer'. There was 'no inherent conflict between growth and performance and safety'. Still, safety began to worry both him and railway inspectors at the Health and Safety Executive. A month after Winsor became Rail Regulator, a Health and Safety report (the Railway Safety Statistics Bulletin 1998–99) showed an alarming increase in the number of broken rails, up by twenty-one per cent on the previous year—937 actual breakages against a Railtrack forecast of 600. On the same day, August 12, he wrote to Gerald Corbett at Railtrack demanding an 'action plan'. A fierce correspondence followed throughout the rest of the year and into 2000. Winsor accused Railtrack of lacking 'effective asset management'. When, on September 1, 1999, Railtrack explained that the increase in broken rails was caused partly by 'rail nearing the end of its life in high tonnage routes', Winsor replied that the spate of rail breaks 'does not seem to suggest that the rail was *nearing* life expiry, but that it was already *at*, or even *beyond* life expiry' [his italics]. Winsor's letters demanded details of likely causes and proposed remedies and suggested that the number of broken rails was prima facie evidence that Railtrack was breaching its government licence to run the infrastructure. In July 2000, Railtrack 'categorically refuted' the allegation that the backlog of track defects had built up because resources were being diverted elsewhere. Winsor and the Health and Safety Executive then looked abroad for expert and independent advice and commissioned an investigation from the Transportation Technology Center in Colorado into Railtrack's method of managing broken rails. The Center produced a very long report, one conclusion of which was that Railtrack should inspect and replace rails more often.

It was published eight days after the Hatfield crash. When the American researchers completed their work, nobody had died because of a broken rail since 1967. But at the curve, sixteen miles up the line from the bureaucratic anger in London, the rail had continued to crack as the letters went back and forth between Winsor and Corbett. Hour after hour, day after day, expresses rode over it at 115 mph.

8. Blame

Many people knew about this cracking rail. In 1999, four years after it had been laid, workers for Balfour Beatty noticed early evidence of gauge corner cracking. Their superiors knew it would have to be replaced eventually—the question was when. Tiny cracks can grow quickly or slowly or not grow at all—aircraft engineers inspecting aircraft frames make similar calculations. In January 2000, a decision was made to replace it. The work would start in May. New rails arrived at the site around this time, but the work didn't start. Unspecified 'difficulties' postponed replacement till November. In September, the rail was treated by grinding by a special machine which wears down the surface and, or this is the intention, removes the cracks.

In the meantime it was inspected, once a week by the human eye of a man walking along the track, ultrasonically once every three months by a machine which rolls along the rail and scans its interior. This, for a high rail on a high-speed curve, was normal practice. By Railtrack's admission, at least one ultrasonic scan was classified as unreadable. An unreadable ultrasonic scan suggests that either the cracking was so extensive that the machine couldn't cope with it, or that the machine didn't work. In either case, a 20 mph speed limit should have been automatically imposed. Even without ultrasonic scanning, all the available evidence suggests that this had been, or should have been, recognized as a most dangerous rail which demanded the imposition of a speed limit. When the rail was reassembled after the crash it bore obvious signs of pre-crash metal distress. Apart from the cracking, its top surface had flaked up to a depth of 3mm. A speed limit would have prevented four deaths.

On the day after the crash, Railtrack admitted that the condition of the rail was 'wholly unacceptable'. Later, before the House of Commons Select Committee on Transport, Gerald Corbett went further and said the rail was in an 'appalling' state. He couldn't understand why a speed limit hadn't been imposed: it was 'either incompetence or a systems failure, or...there might be a cultural aspect to it'. Tom Winsor, the Rail Regulator, concluded that there had been 'almost certainly a failure in the chain of command...between Railtrack and the organization engaged to carry out maintenance on that piece of network'. The Commons committee concluded that it was 'clear that Railtrack's management of Balfour Beatty...prior to October 17 was totally inadequate'.

How much did Balfour Beatty tell Railtrack? What were Railtrack's instructions to Balfour Beatty? Which people are at fault? Who are the guilty men? As I write, in late January, police investigations continue. Witnesses have been reluctant to be interviewed. There are filing cabinets of documents to be read. The evidence may support a criminal prosecution. The public mood, so far as one can tell, would like big fish in the net and the charge of corporate manslaughter. That is unlikely; as someone close to the Hatfield investigation said to me, you would need to find a piece of paper with unlikely words written on it such as *Do not repair this track, we can't afford it, Yrs sincerely The Fat Controller.* More likely is a charge of manslaughter—culpable homicide—made against individuals lower down the management ladder, or their prosecution for a breach of the Health and Safety at Work Act.

Corbett offered his resignation to the Railtrack board on October 18 and had it rejected. Railtrack's management was by now in a shaking fuddle. It had imposed emergency speed restrictions at eighty sites on the previous night and now went on imposing them wherever cracked rails were found. Eventually the number of speed restrictions, some as low as 5 mph, rose to 450. Entire lines sometimes closed for a day or two. Glasgow was cut off from the south. Passengers from London spent twelve hours getting to Nottingham on a journey that should have taken two. Railtrack promised to relay 250 miles of rail and have normality restored by Christmas. At Christmas, normality was postponed to Easter. A National Rail Recovery Plan was announced. The prime minister called 'rail summits' at which heads would be 'knocked together'. On December 12, he conceded that it was 'absolute hell travelling on the railways' and promised that if the situation was not sorted out by January he would use 'the necessary powers...to issue guidance to speed this whole process up'. That was his biggest stick. The growing demand to have the railway infrastructure taken back into public ownership was firmly rejected, though it had supporters (columnists in *The Times* and *Daily Mail*, for example) who had political positions far removed from the prime minister's least favourite word, socialism. Railtrack: who could deny the oddity and scandal of it? It took public money and paid private dividends; it received continual instructions and interference from the government via the Rail Regulator; its revenues were fixed; it couldn't grow; it didn't work. But it had its convenience to governments: in one columnist's words, 'the nationalization of credit and the privatization of blame'. Its chief executive, Gerald Corbett, was interviewed on BBC Television two days after the crash and the day after he'd offered to resign. He said: 'The railways were ripped apart at privatization and the structure that was put in place was a structure designed, if we are honest, to maximize the proceeds to the Treasury. It was not a structure designed to optimize safety, optimize investment or, indeed, cope with the huge increase in the number of passengers the railway has seen.'

On November 10 he gave evidence to the Cullen Inquiry.

Counsel: 'In statements made to the media you have indicated that, in your view, there are fundamental structural flaws in the privatized industry. You have called for a restructuring of the industry in what has been described as a personal manifesto for fundamental change. Indeed, in your own statement, at page 4, paragraph 11, you yourself quote part of an interview that you gave to BBC *Newsnight* on October 19. On another occasion you announced publicly that we have got to think the unthinkable, that we have got to think radically.

'Mr Corbett, all this appears to suggest that there has been a radical change in your view of the structure of the railway and, given that this change appeared to manifest itself post-Hatfield, that the rail at Hatfield was, if you like, a "Road to Damascus". What I want to explore with you is whether that is correct and the degree to which you consider that the problems currently facing the railways are of a fundamental nature, fundamental structural problems?'

Corbett: 'Yes. I do not believe that I have ever come up with a personal manifesto and I do not believe I have ever called for restructuring. I have called attention, though, to some of the tensions and some of the difficulties with the current structure. It is not for me to try and resolve those. I think, though, it is incumbent on me in my role in the industry to draw people's attention to it. I would not describe Hatfield as a damascene conversion because these tensions have been apparent for a while. If you would like me to develop the argument, I will.'

Counsel: 'Please do.'

Corbett: 'The railway as a system, under BR it was totally integrated and one person or group of people were able to balance the system. Performance, safety, efficiency, capacity, growth, it is all one system. I think that privatization did fragment that system into over 100 different parts. That fragmentation did mean that the accountabilities were diffused and many of the different parts were set up with an economic architecture which by definition pointed them in different directions. I think it is the fragmentation and the economic incentives and the lack of clarity of accountability that actually makes it harder now to balance the system than it was then...

'I think a month ago it was unthinkable for Railtrack to contemplate bringing its maintenance in-house. We employ 12,000 people. There is around 18,000 people employed in the maintenance contractors. I think that was an unthinkable thought given the size of the management challenge. But I think now, today, after what happened at Hatfield, we have to seriously review the new form of contract that we have and whether that is going to deliver the safety and the improvements that we all require...

'Let us the start with the maintenance contracts. The maintenance was outsourced on privatization. In 1995 the old British Rail infrastructure systems' companies were broken off. The contracts were agreed that they would maintain the railway to standards and they would get a lump sum of money to do that. That lump sum was based on what was spent on maintenance in the final years of BR and that lump was to decline by three per cent per annum over the next five years. Those were the contracts that we inherited.

'When I arrived at Railtrack at the end of 1997 the assumption was that we had a "competent contractor". No one was able to answer the question: "Which contractors are doing well, which are not?" There were no measures in place. The contractors did not have any specific targets. They had been broken off and that was the situation which we inherited...'

Counsel: 'Has adherence to performance objectives adversely affected your management of safety?'

Corbett: 'I think that answer will only be provided when we have the report on Hatfield. The tragedy at Hatfield, there was a broken rail, the rail was not in acceptable condition. I think we have to understand why speed restrictions were not put on that site. There was a number of opportunities when they could have been and they were not taken. I think when we have the answer to that we will be in a better position to be able to say whether or not the stress on performance has affected the culture at the frontline.'

Lord Cullen: 'Mr Corbett, I have some difficulty with that answer because I would have thought that if there was genuine cause for concern on this subject, that is a challenge for management to tackle the problem [promptly], if it exists?'

Corbett: 'Absolutely.'

Seven days after Corbett gave this evidence, he was sacked by his board and went on holiday to India. His replacement, Steven Marshall, also had a previous career in the financial department of Grand Metropolitan hotels. Railtrack decided that it would not bring maintenance work in-house. On February 1, the Strategic Rail Authority announced that it still had no strategy, though one could be expected by the end of the year. Permanent way engineers were recruited from Romania and India.

9. Punishment

The history of large railway accidents is filled with small human mistakes; these things happen. Signalman James Tinsley, for example. Signalman Tinsley had an arrangement with his colleague, Signalman Meakin, that allowed him to start work ten minutes after his official signing-on time of 6 a.m. In that way he could reach the signal box more conveniently by the first morning train rather than rising from his bed earlier and making the two mile walk. It was a neat arrangement for a signal box in the countryside near the Scottish border; remote from inspectors and managers, a place called Quintinshill. His colleague Meakin would work the extra ten minutes, recording the train movements during those minutes on a scrap of paper which Tinsley would then copy into the official signal box log, preserving the appearance that he had been on duty since six.

On the morning of May 22, 1915, Tinsley was preoccupied with his copying while Meakin chatted to a couple of railwaymen who had come into the box. The First World War was nine months old. The line Meakin and Tinsley controlled was the main route from England to Scotland, busy with trains of troops and naval coal. A northbound local—the train that Tinsley had arrived on—had been shunted by Meakin on to the southbound line to allow a late-running night express from London to overtake it. There it lay outside the box, forgotten. At 6.42, the next signal box to the north indicated to Tinsley that a special train was on its way south. Would Quintinshill accept it? Tinsley set the signals to green. At 6.48, the special came down the gradient at high speed carrying troops of the Royal Scots Regiment bound for Liverpool and the Dardanelles. The special hit the local, then, coming in the opposite direction and also at speed, the night express ran into the wreckage of both. All the carriages were wooden and those of the troop train lit by gas. A great fire at Quintinshill burned for twenty-four hours. Of the 227 dead, all but ten were young men of the Royal Scots.

A Scottish court found Tinsley and Meakin guilty of culpable homicide. Tinsley was sentenced to three years in jail and Meakin to eighteen months, but they were pardoned within a year. Both men had suffered severe nervous breakdowns.

The politicians and their advisers who, in Corbett's phrase, 'ripped apart' Britain's railways have never spoken publicly about the crash at Howe Dell, though sometimes their successors in the Conservative Party have admitted that 'they got some things wrong'. They have directorships, they sit on boards, they have lunch at the club. So far as we know, they sleep soundly at night. A nervous breakdown or two would be just. □

maps money 200 history mud
bites language reliable routes
landscape readable visas cobbles
palms beer informative plan
table moving guidebooks stay
trains leaving dance for barrier
beds eat wine independent entry
bus creek pass minded smell
temple trail dust travellers truck
beach steps cold on airstrip dry
bars ticket song all late wander
dawn province budgets style
swim roads rough good guides

NECESSARY
companions

ROUGH
GUIDES

BURYING
THE EMPEROR
John Ryle

Haile Selassie, seated, with his children, circa 1930

Burying the Emperor

On the twenty-sixth day of Tikimt in the year 1993 (November 5, 2000 in the Gregorian calendar), amid a throng of mourners and onlookers, some of them weeping and kissing the ground in prayer, I watched as the remains of Haile Selassie the First, former Emperor of Ethiopia, were carried from the Ba'ata Mariam Geda church and monastery in Addis Ababa, down towards Meskal Square, the Square of the Finding of the True Cross, for the start of his long-delayed public obsequies. The rainy season was coming to an end; the sky was sharp and blue; the day was hot. Princes and princesses of the blood, bishops and priests and surviving *dejazmatches* and *fitawraris* (the highest officials of the old regime), flanked the coffin. For them the ceremony was a relief. Twenty-five years after his death, His Imperial Majesty, King of Kings, Elect of God, Defender of the Faith—this man of many titles—was finally being laid to rest, though they still could not be certain how he met his end.

For seventeen of the twenty-five years since the Emperor died, the whereabouts of his body had been unknown. During this time it had been buried vertically and sealed in concrete beneath a latrine in the grounds of the Menilek Palace, where he had been imprisoned by the Derg, the military junta that deposed him in 1974. For another eight years, from 1992, after the defeat of the Derg, his exhumed remains were kept in a box inside a glass-fronted case in the crypt of Ba'ata Mariam, near the tomb of his predecessor Menilek the Second. During that time curious visitors like myself could pay a deacon thirty *birr*—four or five US dollars—to be led through a trapdoor into the basement of the church to look at the box, with its tiny portrait of the Emperor holding his staff of office, and a bouquet of dust-laden silk flowers alongside. Meanwhile the surviving members of the royal family argued with the new government, which ousted the Derg from power in 1991, over whether or not he would have a state funeral. Now his bones were finally on their way through the city back to Holy Trinity, the Italianate cathedral built in the 1930s at the Emperor's command, where a granite tomb, carved for him in the style of the monuments of the early medieval rulers of Axum, in the north of Ethiopia, from whom he claimed descent, had been waiting for half a century.

Around nine in the morning—three o' clock in Ethiopia, where

109

John Ryle

the hours are counted from daybreak—the coffin was placed on a flatbed truck draped with flags and banners and floral decorations for the start of its progress round the streets of the city. The hearse was guarded at each corner by former members of the Imperial Bodyguard, veterans of the 1940–1 war against the Italians, the campaign in which Haile Selassie, with assistance from a British Expeditionary Force, expelled Mussolini's invading army, bolstering his reputation as a hero of the anti-fascist movement. The Patriots—the official name for the veterans—some of them now in their eighties, carried seven-foot spears and shields of rhino hide. They wore lion's-mane headdresses and brightly embroidered felt cloaks decorated with campaign medals from the Second World War and the Korean War.

The coffin they were guarding was huge, the biggest anybody in the crowd had ever seen, bigger than any of those displayed outside the undertakers' shops on Churchill Avenue, the main street in Addis Ababa, where the cortège was due to pass later in the day. It was two or three times bigger than the Emperor himself, for Haile Selassie was barely five feet tall. This oversized coffin contained, in fact, the smaller box in which the remains had been placed when they were first disinterred. An enlarged photograph of the Emperor was displayed at the head of the new coffin, his unwavering eyes gazing out over the city. Portraits such as this had once hung in every government office in Addis Ababa. Today, though, was the first time his face had been seen in a public ceremony in Ethiopia for a quarter of a century.

Everyone who saw Haile Selassie was struck by his eyes. The British scholar, Edward Ullendorf, translator of his long but unrevealing autobiography, describes the future emperor as having 'delicate, slender, beautiful hands and imperious eyes'. Haile Selassie's physician in the 1930s, a Frenchman called Sassard, wrote: 'only his eyes seem alive—brilliant, elongated, extremely expressive eyes. They bespeak boredom as well as polite indifference, cold irony, or even anger.'

'The courtiers,' Sassard continued, 'know these different expressions well and retire suddenly when the monarch's glance becomes indifferent, then hard. On the other hand, especially when he is dealing with Europeans, his eyes know how to be soft, caressing, affable—even sincere.'

For four decades, from the 1930s to the 1960s, Ethiopia was defined by the figure of the Emperor, a diminutive autocrat in an outsize sola topi, the canvas-covered hard hat once favoured by British empire-builders. A scion of the royal house of Shoa, one of the highland provinces, his title and given name was Ras Tafari Makonnen. In the 1920s he ousted his rivals and manoeuvred his way to power through court intrigue, marginalizing the feudal lords of the highlands and becoming Haile Selassie, Power of the Trinity, the unchallenged ruler of the Ethiopian empire. It was the only country in Africa uncolonized by any European nation. He was the first Ethiopian ruler to travel abroad. In the words of *Time* magazine, in a backhanded citation for Man of the Year in 1935, he 'rose out of murky obscurity and carried his country with him up and up into brilliant focus before a pop-eyed world'. He had, said *Time*, 'a grasp of both savage and diplomatic mentality, and plenty of what Hollywood calls *It*'.

Haile Selassie's motto as Emperor was a phrase from the Old Testament which prophesied the coming of Christ: 'The Lion of Judah Has Prevailed'. He was very fond of animals, lions in particular—more relaxed with them, according to a German writer who acted as Imperial Librarian, than he was with human beings. In one of the royal palaces there was a menagerie where he kept a pride of tame black-maned Abyssinian lions, feeding them each morning by hand. On churches and public buildings throughout the Empire representations of lions figured prominently.

As ruler of Ethiopia Haile Selassie employed all the devices of tradition and the mystical emblems of kingship, along with an autocratic governing style, in his quest to modernize the country. He began the transformation of the ramshackle empire into a nation state, abolishing slavery, building schools and hospitals and establishing a centralized administration. He argued for Ethiopia's admission to the League of Nations, the precursor of the UN. It was at the League of Nations in Geneva, after Mussolini invaded Ethiopia in 1935, that the Emperor delivered an eloquent speech of protest, the speech that put him on the cover of *Time*. A later speech was to provide the lyric for Bob Marley's reggae anthem 'War': 'Until the philosophy which holds one race superior and another inferior is finally and permanently discredited and abandoned...the dream of lasting peace will remain but a fleeting illusion.' It was Marley who added the words of the refrain: *Everywhere is war.*

Driven out of Ethiopia by the Italians—forced, reluctantly, to leave his lions behind—Haile Selassie went into exile in England, in Bath, where he lived for the next four years. In 1941, restored to the throne with the help of the British, he affirmed his role as a nationalist rallying-point and beacon of anti-fascism. And as an autocrat. An Ethiopian friend of mine keeps a proclamation by the Emperor from the time of the Italian occupation pinned on his wall:

> Everyone will now be mobilized and all boys old enough to carry a spear will be sent to Addis Ababa. Married men will take their wives to carry food and cook. Those without wives will take any woman without a husband. Women with small babies need not go. Those blind, who cannot walk or for any reason cannot carry a spear are exempted. Anyone found at home after receipt of this order will be hanged.

For romantic Europeans Haile Selassie was a perfect combination of modern leader and noble savage, one who had the nous to be on the right side in the clash of the great powers. While for Ethiopians, through political will and force of personality, he became the embodiment of nationhood.

Within Ethiopia, during his reign, government control of the media ensured uncritical respect: the Emperor was lauded as the anointed representative of the ancient Solomonic dynasty, spearhead of progress and, in the post-colonial era, leader among leaders of the newly independent countries of Africa. Only in the 1960s did his reputation falter, as student radicals, the educated elite that he had created, began to criticize the pace of political reform. Internationally his reputation suffered after his attempt to conceal the effects of a famine in the highlands, a fiasco exposed by a BBC film that juxtaposed shots of feasting in the Emperor's palace with starvation in the countryside.

Then, in 1974, Haile Selassie was toppled by a military coup. He became a non-person. His presence was systematically expunged from the capital: streets named after him renamed; statues removed and destroyed (or concealed, as some still are, under dust sheets at the back of the national museum); his image in government offices replaced with that of Mengistu Haile Mariam, the army colonel who was head of the Derg, the Marxist junta that deposed and finally killed him. Only the lions remained.

Outside Ethiopia, however, the name of Haile Selassie was gaining wider currency. The Emperor's reputation as a right-minded African leader had made him fashionable in Europe, but in the African-American political imagination he was accorded a far greater significance. In the ferment of spiritual and political debate in the United States and the Caribbean from the 1930s onwards Haile Selassie's unique position as the monarch of a country uncolonized by Europeans, combined with his claim to be descended in an ancient line from the Kings of Israel, gave his name a unique mythic force.

Among the first to recognize this was the Jamaican-born founder of the Back-to-Africa movement, Marcus Garvey, whose Universal Negro Improvement Association boasted, at its peak, a membership of hundreds of thousands. Garvey is widely credited as the first to make the connection between biblical prophecy and the new ruler of Ethiopia. 'Look to Africa for the crowning of a Black King', he told an audience in the 1920s. 'He shall be the redeemer.' In Garvey's account of Haile Selassie's coronation, he wrote: 'It is for us of the Negro race to assist in every way to hold up the hand of Emperor Ras Tafari.'

Later Garvey changed his mind. Slighted by the Emperor in England, and disillusioned by what he saw as his failure to embrace the global cause of black people, Garvey came to the conclusion that Haile Selassie was not the Messiah at all. He wrote bitter attacks on him, accusing him of espousing slavery and of being the willing puppet of white people. But it was too late. He had sown the seed of a new religion. Even as Garvey lived out his life in exile in England, Rastafarianism was taking shape in the ghettoes of Kingston, with

John Ryle

Haile Selassie as its redeemer and Garvey as its prophet. And when the Emperor made a state visit to Jamaica in 1966 he was surprised to be greeted at the airport by a huge crowd of dreadlocked devotees.

When I first visited Ethiopia in 1982, the only place you could see a picture of Haile Selassie, or find any reference to him at all, was in the homes of Rastafarians in Shashemane, a Rift Valley town where he made land grants available to West Indians seeking a new life in the promised land. There I heard an elderly Jamaican describe his epic journey from the Caribbean, through Europe and North Africa, up the Nile Valley until he reached the Ethiopian border, and the Emperor's fulfilment of his promise to give him a place to make a new home. For the Rastafarians of Shashemane, Haile Selassie was a living God. But in Ethiopia under the Derg, this was not a belief it was wise to advertise.

During the 1970s and 1980s, as post-imperial Ethiopia became a byword for famine and war, the image of the Emperor in the outside world came to be defined by two contradictory texts. On the one hand there was Ryszard Kapuscinski's *The Emperor*, the sardonic account by a Polish journalist of the rituals of palace life during the last days of Haile Selassie's regime, a book in which the Emperor figures as a senile despot presiding over a court of sycophants. On the other there was Bob Marley's Rasta hymnody, the songs that could be heard playing in the evenings in Shashemane, in which the Emperor figures, not as despot, but as Messiah, and which were now broadcasting his name to a global audience.

Today, under the government of Meles Zenawi, the leader of a rebel army from the northern province of Tigray that overthrew the Derg, the name of the Emperor has returned to public discourse in Ethiopia. You can buy a portrait of him in the kiosks that sell religious souvenirs—pictures of the Virgin and the Angel Gabriel. There is a tiny royalist political party, though it has not competed in elections. There is even a local version of reggae, with Amharic lyrics that invoke the Emperor's name against a loping Trenchtown backbeat, with the massed horns of Ethiopian pop in the background. But the leading spirits of the government, some of whom began their insurgency back in the Emperor's time, are a very long way from being monarchists. And politics in Ethiopia remains bitter and unforgiving. There is still no agreement about Haile Selassie, about the meaning of his life or the circumstances of his death. And the Emperor's funeral, far from being the occasion, as some had hoped, for an act of national reconciliation, turned out to be the source of further dissent.

The weeks leading up to it were filled with uncertainty and alarm. While the Emperor's descendants, most of whom live in Europe or Canada or the United States, were gathering in Addis Ababa, the government issued a statement dissociating itself from the ceremony in unequivocal terms. Haile Selassie's reign, the statement ran, was marked by its brutality and extreme oppression of the Ethiopian peasants. The Emperor, the statement continued, was a tyrant who had caused untold misery while amassing a huge personal fortune looted from the people of Ethiopia. This had been deposited in foreign banks; the government was still trying to get it back. An anti-government newspaper, *Menilek*, reported the story under a mocking headline, A THIEF THINKS EVERYONE ELSE IS A THIEF.

Two of the Emperor's grandchildren, Prince Ermias and Prince Bekere, who were visiting their homeland for the first time in twenty-six years, left the country immediately. They were at the airport as I arrived, on their way back to Rome. Prince Ermias said that the government was deliberately neglecting security arrangements for the funeral in order to increase the risk of violence and discourage attendance. But the royal family was divided; other members were determined that the funeral should go ahead. They included Prince Zara-Yakob, the Oxford-educated son of the late crown prince, a troubled soul who lived with Rastafarians in Manchester for a number of years, and his aunt, the octogenarian Princess Tenagne-Worq, only surviving child of the Emperor. Of all the members of the royal family, it was said, the princess was most insistent that the funeral should go ahead.

In Meskal Square the crowd was small. It seemed Prince Ermias might have been right about the government's desire to discourage attendance. There was a smattering of the diplomatic corps, including the ambassadors of South Korea and Togo and the acting British head of mission; there was no sign of the ambassador of the United States, which is one of the Ethiopian government's principal supporters. And although the funeral programme, hastily printed a few days before, announced that there would be an official government representative present, there was none to be seen. Earlier in the day I had been drinking coffee with an Ethiopian colleague at Leyu Muya, a cafe with a panoramic view across Meskal Square, when the Minister of the Interior walked in. He took a discreet look around and departed. Only my companion noticed him. That turned out to be the closest there was to an official presence at the funeral.

Meskal Square, like the rest of Addis Ababa, is haunted by the violence of the Derg. A wide, windswept space designed for rallies and march-pasts, it was the location of Mengistu's most notorious speech. Around the time of Haile Selassie's death he announced a campaign of urban counter-insurgency which he called, with conscious reference to the French and Russian revolutions, the Red Terror. The Red Terror claimed the lives of thousands of young Ethiopians accused by neighbourhood committees of being counter-revolutionary. In Meskal Square Mengistu smashed vials of blood-red liquid on the ground to represent the death of imperialists and renegades, announcing that it would be renamed Revolution Square. Huge North Korean-designed hoardings with portraits of Marx, Engels and Lenin greeted visitors to the country as they drove in from the airport. Further up the hill was a similarly vast and flattering portrait of Mengistu himself. In Addis Ababa, it became clear, one emperor had been substituted for another—Louis XIV had been replaced by Stalin.

It is hard to imagine the brutalizing effect of the Red Terror. It was a time when citizens of Ethiopia might wake in the morning to find the mutilated body of a brother, husband or son lying in the street with a sign pinned to it saying: I WAS AN ANARCHIST or I BETRAYED THE REVOLUTION. To reclaim the body, the family of the victim would then have to apply to the local revolutionary committee. Sometimes they would be required to pay the cost of the bullet. They were the lucky ones, who managed to get the bodies of their relatives back. Many corpses were not recovered until after the fall of the Derg, in the spate of disinterments which included the Emperor's. In a country where the rituals that surround death are of paramount importance— the Ethiopian church prescribes forty days of prayer for the dead—the Derg banned mourning. A relative of a victim of the Red Terror told me that a keening committee had been organized secretly by mothers of the dead, its name—the *u-u-ta* committee—echoing the ululation of grief-stricken women. One mother would start and another would carry on, until the sound of crying was heard in every home. This sound, it seemed to me, could still be heard in Meskal Square.

Today the Square is empty, stripped of Communist icons. Its original name has been restored. A tiny stone plinth, scarcely the size of a tombstone, commemorates those who lost their lives in the Terror. There is no monument to the Emperor. The present Prime Minister of Ethiopia, Meles Zenawi, has eschewed the personality cult as practised both by Mengistu and by Haile Selassie. It is hard to find a picture of him anywhere in the city. Although there are undoubtedly more freedoms in Ethiopia today than there were under the Derg—more, some would say, than there were under the Emperor—the style of politics has not changed: the government does not engage with its critics. There is no national dialogue. And the government is not popular in the capital. Its leading figures hail from elsewhere in the country, from Tigray to the north. The Amhara elite, native to Addis Ababa, accustomed to wielding authority, feels disenfranchised. There is a void in the life of the city, as though power itself had fled. Meles Zenawi himself described this phenomenon to me when I interviewed him some years ago. 'Politics in this country was essentially armed politics,' he said. 'You didn't win through arguments, through logic, you won through shooting straighter than the other guy. So victories and defeats were to a large extent total.

'And even if they were not total,' the Prime Minister continued, 'they were perceived to be total. That does not encourage compromise.'

And there is the war. A two-year war with Eritrea ended in an uneasy peace last year, leaving tens of thousands of casualties and extensive displacement from the border areas. The war produced a brief surge of nationalism, but it has sapped the economy of the country. Famine threatens again in the highlands and the streets of Addis Ababa are filled with ever-increasing numbers of desperate homeless people: street children, war veterans and indigent peasants. Addis, despite its astonishingly beautiful setting in a bowl of hills, is a dispiriting place, barely a hundred years old but with the air of a medieval city, with reeking tin-shack slums huddled below the palaces and grand municipal buildings. Beggars grab your sleeve everywhere you go, or tap on the window of your taxi, crying 'Hungry!', 'Stomach Zero!', 'Father! Give me bread!' The city is over 7,000 feet above sea level; after dark it can be very cold. A recent study reported that almost half the inhabitants lacked proper housing. To walk in the streets at midnight reveals scenes of profound misery, people seeking shelter in hedges and ditches, with no blankets or firewood, fighting with feral dogs for sleeping space.

The only recent event to cause unequivocal celebration has been the victory in the Olympics of the long-distance runner Haile Gabre-Selassie. His face is now the most recognizable in the country. I met him in Meskal Square, a genial man, as self-effacing as it is possible to be with a seven-storey portrait of yourself soaring up the side of an office building across the road. His return from Sydney with the 10,000 metre gold medal had been, by all accounts, a much bigger event than the Emperor's funeral. My Ethiopian colleague, not unsympathetic to the government, said that by boycotting the funeral it was missing a similar chance for good publicity. Having permitted the event to go ahead, he said, the Prime Minister could have claimed the credit for it instead of allowing the government spokesman to pour cold water on the whole thing. He said, 'This was not a mistake the Emperor would have made.'

But the government may have been studying the demographics. It is over twenty-five years since the Emperor died. Most Ethiopians are under that age. For them the name of Haile Selassie means very little—much less, probably, than that of the other Haile, the Olympic athlete. Young adults in Ethiopia today grew up in a time when the Emperor was written out of the history books, as he still is, to a greater or lesser extent. In a textbook that I picked up at random in the Mega bookshop off Meskal Square, a retail chain associated with the ruling party, his reign is covered in just three or four paragraphs. An acquaintance of my Ethiopian colleague who lived through the

Red Terror was in despair over this loss of communal memory. During the funeral procession, one of the street children who harass passers-by accosted him and said: 'So, you bald old man, why are you bothering with this Haile Selassie? Has he not been dead for a long time?' I asked him how he had responded. He said he could not feel anger. He just said to the boy: 'I hope you do not live to see the days that I have seen.'

In Meskal Square the Emperor's cortège was leaving at high speed. The organizers were nervous about the government's reluctance to provide them with a full escort. It passed the football stadium and headed up Churchill Avenue, the main street of Addis Ababa, past the National Theatre and the Black Lion hospital and the post office, all buildings that had been constructed in the Emperor's time. It halted at the top of the hill, for a mass at St George's Church. The Emperor had been crowned here seventy years before, in a ceremony whose pageantry marked the dawn of his international celebrity. The coronation was covered for *The Times* by Evelyn Waugh, who later lampooned it in his novel *Black Mischief.* It took up sixty pages in the *National Geographic.* Faint echoes of the coronation spirit could be seen in the gaudy uniforms of the war veterans as they stood to attention alongside the hearse. But the moment passed. The cortège turned eastwards, skirting the lion park, where a dozen mangy specimens, said to be descendants of the original imperial pets, can still be seen, and headed back down towards the cathedral, where the patriarch of the Ethiopian Church was preparing to perform the final ceremony. Here the cortège slowed down to negotiate the narrow approach to the cathedral, which is sandwiched between two modern buildings, the parliament and the politburo. It drew to a halt in the forecourt, where the Patriarch, Abuna Paulos, was enthroned on the steps with the mourners assembled around him. Priests and deacons with velvet parasols crowded the forecourt. Keening women were straining at the barriers round the church, photographers were climbing on the statues of the evangelists outside the building in search of a better camera angles; foreign reporters were rushing around in search of translators for Amharic and for Ge'ez, the liturgical language of the Ethiopian Church (as distinct from Amharic

John Ryle

as Latin is from Italian). Some of the journalists had scribbled
genealogical diagrams in their hands, trying to relate them to the
royal mourners, wondering whether or not they had been
interviewing the right prince.

The royal family, dressed in black, were sitting in a line: Princess
Tenagne-Worq, her nephews and nieces and great-nephews and great-
nieces. They formed a living diagram, if you could decipher it, of the
Solomonic dynasty, the lineage of which Haile Selassie claimed to be
the 225th representative. The perfectly dressed princes in their silk ties
and handkerchiefs, their Savile Row suits and dove-grey Homburgs,
brought a suggestion of the Emperor's court to the proceedings, a
glimpse of a vanished milieu, of the era, one of them said, when it
had still been possible to feel optimistic about Ethiopia's future. Some
of the young princesses were very beautiful. It was hard, though, not
to see this as the last gasp of the dynasty. The Emperor's features were
not reflected in their faces. The younger members of the royal family
have lived outside Ethiopia all their lives. A number work in public
relations, a skill they may have inherited from their grandfather. They
have come to resemble the disinherited royal families of Europe, with
little to distinguish them from the haute bourgeoisie.

The Patriarch spoke. He discussed the role of the Emperor in
the church, in the history of the country, the cruel manner of his
death. There were murmurs of approbation. Abuna Paulos is from
Tigray and assumed to be a supporter of the government; for the
royals, his unambiguous praise for the Emperor in Ethiopia's
uncompromising political climate came as a pleasant surprise.

Soon the priests began to dance, a feature of Ethiopian church
rituals that re-enacts the biblical King David dancing before the Ark
of the Covenant (the Emperor being, according to his Solomonic
pedigree, descended from the House of David). The photographers
climbed further up the statues of the evangelists; the journalists
consulted their translators. Finally, the giant coffin was carried
inside the cathedral and up the aisle to a screened area where the
tomb was open to receive it. Princess Tenagne-Worq took the flag
that covered it; the pall-bearers prepared to lower it into the tomb.
But there was a last-minute hitch. The coffin would not fit.
Stonemasons had to be called to chip away the cavity to make room

for the coffin. In death, it seemed, the Emperor was still a greater figure than the tomb could hold.

For one group of mourners this did not matter, because they did not believe the Emperor was there at all. Rastafarians, by definition, do not believe that Haile Selassie is dead, though this did not stop a few of them attending his funeral. Most prominent among these was Rita Marley, Bob Marley's widow, every inch the *grande veuve* in an extravagantly gold-embroidered Ethiopian dress, dreadlocks piled high and wrapped in purple velvet. I asked her whether she thought the Emperor was actually dead. She began to sing. 'Like Bob say,' she murmured, *'It not an end, it a new beginning.'*

Later I talked to a British-born Rastafarian, Ambrose King, who works as a building engineer in Addis Ababa and acts as international liaison officer of the Ethiopian World Federation, an organization founded in New York in the 1930s with the aim of promoting the repatriation of African Americans to Ethiopia.

'This is the third time they tried to bury these bones,' said Mr King. 'The first time, in 1992, there were reports that a thousand Rastas were coming to the funeral, but Rastas stay away, then and now. If there is a body lost for seventeen years and you find this body it's a natural thing to do tests and things. But they don't. No one saw him die; no one saw him buried; and no one do any DNA test. So we do not believe it is him.'

When the funeral was over I walked back towards the Menilek Palace, where the Emperor had died. He might have found his final resting place, but in legal terms his death remains an unsolved crime. In a courtroom on the other side of the city, members of the Derg are currently on trial, charged with a range of offences that include his death. Here, from time to time, fragments of evidence are presented that add to the picture of his last days. From testimonies in the trial, now in its seventh year, it is possible to construct a more detailed account of the event.

The Menilek Palace, named after Haile Selassie's predecessor, founder of the city of Addis Ababa, is a rambling collection of Ottoman-style wooden and Italianate stone buildings on a hill in the heart of the city. The word 'palace' is misleading: the random distribution of the buildings reveals its origin as a military encampment, a role it reverted to under the Derg, where it served as a prison and torture centre. It is a gloomy place, overshadowed by pines and cypresses and the ubiquitous bluegum trees of Addis, eucalypts introduced during Menilek's reign as a source of firewood, an innovation that enabled him to make the city his permanent capital. On the summit of the hill is a colonnaded building known from its shape as the Egg House, from where Menilek used to survey the city with a telescope. This is where Haile Selassie spent much of his working life, and where he spent his last days. The palace is still the centre of power in Ethiopia, inaccessible to those not on high government business. In 1995 I visited it in the company of one of Haile Selassie's former court officials, a man who had been imprisoned there for six years under the Derg. He showed me the site on the north side where the Emperor had been buried and the pavilion where he had passed his final days. And he showed me the meeting room of the Derg (a word which means 'committee') where the Emperor's fate had been decided.

What happened on the night of August 25, 1975? In the press coverage of the funeral, the most popular adjective was still 'mysterious'. Although it is widely accepted that he was killed, the event has been surrounded for years by rumour and invention. The official announcement of the death of the ex-Emperor, as he was referred to by the Derg, appeared in a single column in the government newspaper at the end of August 1975. It ascribed his death to circulatory failure. In Addis Ababa, a city where no one believes government announcements and where rumour travels faster than light, it was immediately assumed that he had been done away with. It was said that the killers and the witnesses had all themselves been killed. And that those who killed them had been killed in their turn. Or, alternatively, that the man who killed the Emperor by strangling and kicking him was still alive and living clandestinely in Kenya.

None of these stories, it now seems, was quite true. For a start, there was clearly someone who knew where the body was buried. When the officials of the new regime took over the Menilek Palace in 1991 they were told where they could find the Emperor's body, as they were told where they could find the bodies of other victims of the Red Terror. Accounts of these exhumations formed part of the evidence at the Derg trial when it began in 1994. I attended the first weeks of the trial with a lawyer named Teshome Gabre-Mariam, who had been Attorney-General in the imperial administration. He had been a witness at the exhumation of the Emperor's body. It was the first time since the announcement of his death that the Emperor's name had been uttered in official discourse.

'His Imperial Majesty, Haile Selassie, King of Kings, The Lion of Judah Shall Conquer', the judge began, 'was murdered in a cruel and disgraceful manner, suffocated in his bedchamber.' There was a hush in the courtroom. In the recess Teshome stared at the Derg members as they filed back into the courtroom. 'Ah,' he said. 'Murder the Emperor! A man of eighty-three! What was the point? They have no honour.'

Teshome had been a prisoner in the Menilek Palace when the Emperor was killed. He had narrowly escaped death himself. He told me how he had been arrested with other government officials in 1974 and incarcerated in the basement beneath the Derg's meeting room, near the iron-roofed pavilion where the Emperor was held incommunicado. On November 23, 1974, in the evening, guards came to the basement and called out the names of forty-seven ministers and military officers, a group that a US diplomat at the time described as 'our guest list for the Fourth of July celebration'. Teshome described how he and the other prisoners watched through a small window as their colleagues were driven away from the palace. Later they learned how the imperial officials, with a dozen others who had been held elsewhere, fifty-nine in all, were taken to the central prison, the same prison where the Derg are now held, and lined up against a floodlit wall, the outer wall of an electrocution chamber that had just been installed by the Emperor. There soldiers raked them with machine gun fire. They were buried the next day in a trench.

The Emperor was related to at least half of the fifty-nine. And their fate was a foretaste of his. He, too, was arrested, then driven from his office at the Jubilee Palace with his poodle, Lulu, in a Volkswagen, so that he would not be recognized: the King of Kings and his lapdog, riding for the first and last time in the people's car.

Eight months later, on August 25, 1975, soldiers of the Derg came to his quarters in the Palace and ordered his servants to leave. It was the last they saw of him. In court over twenty years later, one of these servants, now an old man himself, described how the eighty-three-year-old monarch wept and prayed when he realized he was going to be killed. The court translator used an archaic form of words, corresponding, perhaps, to the antique Amharic diction of the witness. According to him the servant heard his master say, 'Is it not true, Ethiopians, that I have strived for you?' Then, he told the court, 'The Emperor sprinkled the floor with his tears. He knelt down and wept and started praying. He understood that it was the end of his days.'

A second palace servant, a man named Eshetu, said he was ordered by guards to leave the room adjoining the Emperor's where he normally slept. 'The next morning,' he said, 'I knocked on his bedroom door and opened it. There was an unusual odour and his face was black.' The Emperor's bedclothes, he added, were not his usual ones; and there was a bandage around his neck. Finally a third witness, a maintenance worker at the palace, described how security officials ordered him to dig not one but four graves in the grounds that morning, so that it would not be known which of them contained the body. Others said that Mengistu came to the palace and inspected the Emperor's corpse.

No autopsy was performed. The Emperor's physician, Asrat Woldeyes, was not called to the palace in time to observe the death. He told the court: 'The day his death was announced, I received a phone call from the Derg office asking me to go to the office of Colonel Mengistu Haile Mariam. I saw that Colonel Mengistu seemed angry, then we were informed that there would be no interview and we could leave.' Professor Asrat, a leading figure in the opposition to the current government of Ethiopia, who himself died in May 1999, soon after he gave this account, did not believe the deposed emperor had died naturally. He testified: 'Despite an operation on the prostate a few months before his death, His Majesty was in excellent health.' According to those who spoke to him outside the court, Ato Eshetu, the Emperor's servant, believed that Haile Selassie had been asphyxiated, suffocated with an ether-soaked pillow. In death, he said, elaborating his statement to the court, 'the Emperor's face looked like granite. There were blue spots on his skin.'

No one has been named as the Emperor's murderer and the prosecution has not produced any evidence to show that there had been a formal decision taken to end his life. A Norwegian journalist, Einar Lunde, citing a former Derg member, Major Negash Tesfatsion, maintains that it was indeed decided by a formal vote of the Derg. But another of the defendants in the Derg trial, Fikre-Selassie Weg-Deres, the former prime minister and Mengistu's second-in-command, denies this. When I interviewed him in prison after the start of his trial, he maintained that there was no evidence that the Emperor was killed. It was not the subject of a meeting, he said. 'We don't believe that he was killed. We believe he died a natural death. He was an old man. There was no danger from him.' Fikre-Selassie's statement, of course, serves his interests as a defendant. It is only notable because he acknowledges the Derg's responsibility for other deaths at the time, including the decision to execute the fifty-nine.

Only one man knows the entire truth, and Mengistu Haile Mariam, leader of the Derg throughout its bloodstained history, is unlikely to break his silence. After his fall Mengistu was given sanctuary by President Mugabe of Zimbabwe. He has lived ever since in a guarded villa in the suburb of Gun Hill in Harare, where he has survived at least one assassination attempt. The condition of his domicile in Zimbabwe is that he does not speak for publication, though he has broken this injunction on at least one occasion. I tried calling him several times from Addis Ababa, the last time from Meskal Square on a borrowed mobile phone, but there was no answer in Gun Hill.

The trial of the Derg continues today in Addis Ababa. It has been riven with delays and procedural irregularities. At one point the Special Prosecutor was himself arrested and jailed for contempt of court. It seems unlikely that the prosecution has any more significant evidence to present. When the Emperor's body was exhumed the royal family refused to submit it to examination, perhaps because of an old superstition that if the body of the monarch was tampered with other members of the family would die. Now that the Emperor has been buried there will never be an autopsy or a DNA test. In this sense,

John Ryle

Ambrose King is right: there is no proof that the body is the Emperor's. Unless the perpetrator himself comes forward, or unless Mengistu Haile Mariam, in his refuge in Zimbabwe, has a sudden attack of conscience, it seems that this account of the Emperor's death is all that posterity is likely to have. Not enough to convince a Rastafarian, but enough for most other people to conclude that Haile Selassie's end was not by natural means.

Before I left the city I paid a visit to the national museum to see another celebrated skeleton, that of the earliest hominid, the oldest human ancestor, Lucy. Lucy, or Denkinesh as she is known to Ethiopians, lived three million years ago. She was dug up by a team of American and Ethiopian palaeoanthropologists in 1974, shortly before the Emperor was killed and buried in Addis. A cast of her bones lies in the basement of the museum, a splay of ribs, vertebrae, and skull fragments. In one sense her fate is the antithesis of the Emperor's. While his remains are now inviolate, sealed from the public gaze, Lucy's have been studied and tested to extract every ounce of meaning. It turns out, though, that Lucy is probably not our oldest ancestor. Other, older hominid remains have been found recently, in Chad and in Ethiopia itself. The story of human evolution, like that of the Solomonic dynasty, is still a little vague.

Haile Selassie's burial may mark the end of the monarchical idea as a force in Ethiopian history. The age of kings is over; monarchs are an endangered species worldwide. Only the kings of Thailand and Cambodia and Nepal and the Emperor of Japan still have a whiff of mystical authority about them. But the Emperor's burial does not mean that his life will cease to be subject to scrutiny. Rather it releases him simultaneously into the realms of history and mythology. Haile Selassie's biographer, Harold Marcus, is finally due to finish his long-awaited work this year. Meanwhile web sites devoted to the Emperor's divinity or obscure claims to his throne are multiplying. Whether it is the forensic gaze of the court, or the mythopoetic magnifying lens of the Rastafarians, or the patient documentary attentions of biographers and historians, the memory of the Emperor, a man who was too big for his tomb, will not lie undisturbed. □

LOVELY GIRLS,
VERY CHEAP
Decca Aitkenhead

The Oriental Hotel in Bangkok is proud of its aristocratic past. It describes itself as colonial, though Thailand has never been a colony, and is staffed by bellboys in magnificent pantaloons who wring their hands when they bow. We arrived there on our first night in Thailand and were immediately presented with personalized gold embossed stationery, so that we could write letters to prove to our friends that we had stayed at the Bangkok Oriental.

The bar was a hushed, burgundy room, and that evening a jazz band was playing. A young Thai woman sheathed in sequins sang Western love songs, and from every table middle-aged white couples watched in silence. The women sipped cocktails through straws, holding their glasses with both hands, never taking their eyes off the band. The men leaned backwards, arms locked straight out in front, palms flat, and from time to time their heads would swivel, as though every one of them was stranded on a blind date that was not working out. We took a table and ordered a Mai Tai. Its arrival was noted by one of the men, and his face lit up in delight.

'Eh, that looks good. What's that one then? A what?' He studied his cocktail menu, then held it up for us, pointing. 'We had this one last. This one's next on my list.' My husband took a sip of his Mai Tai, and the man practically leaped out of the sofa.

'Eh, when I saw that I thought, oh, he's spoiling the wife. But it's for him! And she's got a lemonade, and you've got that!' He laughed and laughed, shaking his head. When he'd subsided he leaned across to Paul. 'Beer man normally, are you?'

Satisfied, he went on, 'When did you get in? We got in this morning. Saw the King's palace. It's definitely not to be missed. Full of lots of different cultures. Different influences. Thai influences...' There was a long pause. 'Um, Cambodian. Very spectacular. Then we went to Papong.' His wife was perched stiffly at right angles to the conversation. She was small, with a frosted blonde hood of hair, and didn't shift or turn her head. 'Patpong,' she corrected softly.

'Yeah, Patpong. Anyway, market were 'eaving, absolutely 'eaving. But it weren't as bad as what I'd thought it would be.' Patpong is Bangkok's famous red-light district. If he'd thought the vice would be bad, I wondered why he'd wanted to go there. 'But the shopping were amazing. We saw this bag,'—his wife wordlessly produced a fake Prada handbag—'and we got the price right down to four hundred baht. Didn't we, love?' He talked us through the haggle like a fisherman reliving how he landed a shark, while his wife murmured, 'You've got to be hard.' She repeated it to herself. 'You've just got to be hard.'

Four hundred baht, at sixty-five to the pound, is roughly equivalent to six pounds, or nine dollars.

'And it's flame resistant!' cried the man, and she held it up like a magician's assistant, and lit a match to it for us to see.

'Normally we go to the Caribbean,' he went on. 'This is our first time East. The wife likes cocktails, you see, so we thought, well, let's go to Fooket. Eh, where are you going?' Paul told him we were aiming for Ko Samui and Ko Pha-Ngan, and he looked momentarily thrown.

'So you're on a three-centre holiday, then? Bangkok, Ko Samui, and—and the other one. Phew.'

We flew south the next day. I had heard about Thailand for most of my adult life, but not of a fallen tiger economy feasted on by herds of package tourists. Friends had described Ko Samui as a hedonist's wonderland, and its neighbour, Ko Pha-Ngan, as a place of dreamy charm. Ko Pha-Ngan had become famous for its Full Moon rave, said by some to be a quasi-spiritual experience. In the course of the Nineties it had assumed the status of Mecca for the Ecstasy generation.

Thus it was that Paul and I found ourselves landing in a small clearing of palm trees later that afternoon. We had undertaken a sort of Ecstasy pilgrimage across the globe in order that I should write a travel book about clubbing, and the trail had naturally led us to Ko Samui. Paul had spent a week there ten years ago, before the gap year or *The Beach* had been invented, and stayed in a town called Chaweng. He remembered it as rustic and charming.

The airport taxi let us out in a resort that looked like Magaluf, Majorca. It had a main strip—two miles of potholed road running parallel to the beach—lined with concrete restaurants and shops, and pubs with names such as Fawlty Towers. Neon signs advertised PUB GRUB, cold beer in a PINT GLASS, and WESTERN TOILETS FOR THE LADIES. On one side of the strip, short muddy tracks led off to collections of bungalows that sprawled down to the beach. Some were built of wood rather than breeze blocks, and we chose the first one with a vacancy. An Italian with a shiny pink head was in charge; he called himself Papa, and showed us to our bungalow, a single creaky room only inches larger than the bed, with sheets of wallpaper for carpet. We unpacked as night fell and then set off back up the track through the dark.

'Hello, welcome! Welcome, hello! Hello, welcome!' As we turned the corner and stepped into the neon glare of the strip, about a dozen young Thai women came running at us. They bumped into each other as they pulled up a yard short, and some clasped each other's shoulders and pretended to double up in giggles, like teenage girls on a dare, astonished at their own audacity. They pointed at a small bar behind them. 'Come! Come!' Twenty yards further down the street this happened again, and then again, and then again. Some of the girls wore tight jeans and halter-neck tops, and others wore little Lycra dresses, but all of them had long glossy hair, which they tossed from side to side, and laughing kitten eyes with which they pleaded. They were stationed at the entrance to every bar, and when we walked past they spilled off their stools and took a run at us. 'Hello, welcome! Hello! Where you from?'

It is a tribute to them that they could make themselves heard at all. Trance and techno blasted out from the bars, and car horns seemed never to stop blaring, but still the cries of 'Welcome!' triumphed, and every few yards a new troop of girls came charging out. The assault was so relentless that we were a good way down the strip before we noticed anything else. Westerners streamed past us, but they were not the backpackers we'd expected to see, yet they didn't look quite like tourists, either, and then it dawned on us that this was because they were all men.

If we really had been in Majorca, they would have been about eighteen. Instead, these men were twenty years older, with grey faces, cropped hair and purple smudges under their eyes. At eighteen they would have have been light on their feet with a suggestion of violence, but these men carried themselves heavily. They wore regulation sportswear and looked like discreet criminals. They filled the pubs and restaurants, drinking slowly and deliberately, and on their laps sat Thai bar girls.

We walked on, startled into silence, past bars called Black Jack and O'Malleys showing premiership football, and then a tattoo parlour (TEN YEARS EXPERIENCE, NEW NEEDLE). There were videos showing in every restaurant and the amplified soundtracks poured on to the street and curdled in the racket, so that it sounded as if we were walking through a gigantic amusement arcade. Several pharmacies were open, doing a brisk trade despite the late hour. They looked like little old-fashioned sweet shops, except that they had posters in the windows offering CLEAN WOUND. PREG TEST.

We stopped for a drink and noticed two men sitting in the next-door bar, both in their early thirties and unmistakably English. One looked amiable enough—dirty blond, with a boxer's nose—but the other had bulging eyes and pumping cheeks and his whole face was working, sending ripples of fat and sweat down his belly. You couldn't say he was smiling—his mouth was too busy to form any definite expression—but his face was a billboard of enjoyment. Both of them were emptying what looked like brown glass medicine bottles into their mouths. I asked what was in them and the fat man hurled himself at the conversation.

'Picks you right up when you've 'ad a few, an' you're spinning, like. Down one of these and you're fackin' bang right, innit? Sorts you right out. Look,' and he pointed to the list of ingredients printed in Thai on the label. 'All herbal, innit? Really good for you stuff, healthy like. Herbs and stuff. Look, it's only 0.5 amphetamine.'

'So it's not speed, then?' Paul asked doubtfully.

'Nah,' he said. 'I had about ten last night. Proper good.' His friend nodded happily. A few minutes later he mentioned that they hadn't been to sleep for four days.

The fat man was called Sean. He was from Reigate and he had been in Chaweng for a few weeks. He had friends waiting for him on another island, but bad weather had prevented the ferry from running, so here he was, stuck on Ko Samui, a state of affairs that didn't seem to trouble him. Eight bar girls were gathered around his stool.

'You come in 'ere,' he exclaimed, gesturing to the bar, 'and they look after you like a prince. They get a wet towel, they wipe yer face... 'Ere!' He summoned the barmaid to give Paul a wet towel. 'I tell you, these girls do everyfing for you.' How much does everything cost, I asked. 'Five hundred baht and they do everyfing. They'll do'—he took a deep breath—'your nails, they'll barf you, do your toenails, clean your hotel room. Everyfing! They're diamonds. Mind you, this one here,' and he nodded, 'she keeps saying, "I love you".' He pulled a disgusted face, shoved her away, then gathered up another into a noisy, wet kiss. All the girls beamed.

'This is Sue,' he went on. 'Sue's a nanny from Bangkok, down here on holiday. Well, I wasn't to know that, was I? I say, "How much?" She says, "Nuffing—I ain't a bar girl, it's for *free*".' His eyes popped even wider. '*Fa*-ckin' ree-*sult*!' Sean couldn't keep still for the wonder of it all, and swayed clean off his stool twice in the telling.

We bought a round of drinks. A few of the girls sneaked cocktails on to the order and Sean exploded in the fashion of a man never happier than when a friend has been slighted. He pretended to shoot the bar girls. He seemed to have developed a proprietorial role towards them, but presently he explained that in fact the Thai man at the door looked after them. 'And 'e won't touch them cos he's *bent*. It's ideal, innit?' Sean gazed about him. His eye fell on his friend, who was now shadow-boxing alone in the corner. 'Diamond geezer, diamond geezer. Wouldn't hurt a fly.'

'Ever been to Goa?' he asked suddenly. 'Now that's cheap, that's fackin' cheap. Beer, 30p! And the Es! Fack me. If you've got the money, get yourself on a plane to Goa, I'm tellin' you. Cheap or fackin' what?' The memory of Goa's prices temporarily silenced him, and in the pause Paul said that we'd wondered about the Ecstasy situation here. Sean was off again.

'Five hundred, mate! Five fackin' hundred.' Overflowing with happiness, he explained that he had smuggled 500 Es in with him. He'd packed them into hollow plastic balls found inside Kinder eggs, a hundred to a ball, and secreted them in his rectum. He mimed the act, indicating chronic pain all the way up to his chest and hopping from foot to foot. I asked if he was selling them in clubs here. 'You fink I'm mad? One hit and I'm done, mate. I'll sell the lot to a dealer, and see how long the money lasts. They're wicked, mind. You can have a couple if you like.' He glanced down and noticed the size of the camera on Paul's arm.

'You're not from the papers are you?' he asked. 'You're not from the *Sun?*' and he roared with laughter, then turned and gathered up another girl for an almighty kiss. From where I was standing, it looked as if he'd simply bent down and eaten her up.

A bar girl in Ko Samui is employed to attract customers. Almost every bar has at least one girl, and some of the larger bars have up to twenty. You don't see them during the day. This is when they sleep. But by sundown they are back in place on their high stools, ready for another long night. 'Come, come!' they beckon, on just the right side of insistence, thereby ensuring that the effect is girlishly charming rather than sluttish. And come men do, with faces full of wolfish delight at the joy of this amazing arrangement which lets them make believe they are sexually appealing.

The overall impression is more naughty school girl than call girl, and this is no accident, because 'of course', as everyone will tell you, 'they are not prostitutes'. The girls' official job description is notionally innocent. They are paid a percentage of the price of every drink that is bought by a customer whom they entice in and entertain. The longer they can keep the customer happy, the more drinks he will buy, and the more the girls will earn. To this end, they fawn and swoon over the men, who can grope and fondle them, sit them on their laps, and bore them to tears with conversation; wisely, the girls have come up with an inventive deterrent to the latter by playing endless games of Kerplunk or backgammon with their partners instead.

This is the basic system. However, if a man wants to take a girl off and have sex with her, all he has to do is pay the bar a fine of about four pounds, and agree a price with the girl. This money she is allowed to keep. More popular than the one-off transaction, which costs ten to twenty pounds all-in, is to start what the men refer to as a 'relationship'. Under this arrangement, the bar girl becomes a 'girlfriend' for the duration of the man's stay—a tirelessly devoted, obliging girlfriend, and a distinct improvement, you might say, on the real thing. In return, the man buys her meals and clothes and so on, as well as presents for her family—in theory her parents, but in practice usually her children, since most bar girls end up in the profession because they are single mothers. So Ko Samui is full of fat and unattractive European men driving around on mopeds with beautiful young Thai women on the back.

There are obvious difficulties in trying to calculate how much a bar girl earns. A recent Thai university survey put the national monthly average for a 'sex worker' at $125, but a Patpong bar girl can earn $150–$200 a month directly from the bar where she works, plus twenty dollars or more per session for sex with private clients. If she strikes lucky with a generous 'boyfriend', there is no limit to what he might give her. Compared to the official per capita income in Bangkok of $580, these sums are still relatively modest, but most bar girls are young, uneducated, and come from rural villages where the legal minimum wage can be as low as three dollars a day. Even in Bangkok, it is only four dollars a day. A hot meal of egg and noodles from a pavement food trolley will cost less than the equivalent of fifty cents, even in a touristy part of town, which means the bar girls are relatively wealthy—though nowhere near as wealthy as the average foreign tourist, who spends a hundred dollars in Thailand every day.

Tourists in Chaweng hadn't a bad word to say about the bar girls. How could they, the girls made everybody feel so good about themselves. The men felt irresistible and went around with faces stuffed with self-congratulation. Their mood was so good, they found themselves behaving nicely to one another, and this novelty put them in a better mood still. They were positively gallant towards white women, who in turn were delighted to be spared the usual advances.

There weren't many white women in Chaweng. Occasionally we would see young European backpackers, stopping off en route to other islands, but most of the women were older and came in groups with their husbands and boyfriends—big beery gangs, on holiday for a month or two. The women made a great fuss of getting along with the bar girls. At night, they would dance on the tables with them, curl their bodies together, laughing. In the day they could be heard remarking loudly on how pretty this or that one looked. Being seen to be sisterly was very important, although it was never clear if this was meant to be read as compassion, or as proof that they felt no sexual threat. Either way, they were thrilled that the girls smiled back, and took it to mean that they liked them.

The only club in Chaweng still open beyond two in the morning would usually run on until dawn, jammed and chaotic. Empty, it would have been a more sophisticated venue than most, with elegant open-air terraces and wicker tables softly lit by lanterns. It was never empty, though, but jammed and chaotic, full of bar girls who came along after their own establishments closed, hoping to pick up some late freelance business. In the crush as we were sitting down, one accidentally put her cigarette out on the tail of a Dalmatian dog that had wandered in from the street. Then another with legs like pipe cleaners pushed past us and vomited into a pot plant. The man sharing our table didn't notice either mishap, for his eyes were locked on two others dancing on stage in lime-green bikinis.

'Lovely girls,' he murmured dreamily.

'What, the prostitutes?' Paul asked. The man turned, shocked.

'Prostitutes? They're not prostitutes. They're bar girls.' And he looked angry, as if Paul had just insulted him.

This would happen whenever anyone said the word prostitute. The men on holiday in Chaweng thought the girls were so lovely, the least one could do was lie about what they did for a living. This lie was to protect the girls' honour, and there was never any doubt that it was the girls who would be shamed by the truth. Their unflagging loveliness made it easy for everyone to uphold the consensus of deceit; nevertheless, at some level the men knew it wasn't true, and so liked to feel that their lie was chivalrous.

The chivalry had its limits. Later that night a scuffle broke out between one of the lime-green-bikini girls, and a stocky German. He slapped her, she bristled, everyone stared—and then she gave a short, tired shrug and walked away. Nobody intervened on her behalf—and in the many similar scenes we witnessed afterwards, nobody ever did.

We quickly stopped noticing the girls, but I became obsessed with the men, and took to quizzing them in the street. Paul thought I was mad and left me to it, but at first I didn't get far because I kept meeting Belgians and Germans, who were polite but offered only pidgin clichés. Then one evening I was sitting in a cafe when a man leaned across and asked: 'Would you like to join us? You are by yourself.' He had his arms around a bar girl, and was smiling broadly. I smiled back.

Rory was a handsome Australian in his mid-thirties. He pulled out a chair and shook my hand.

'And is this your girlfriend?' I said.

'Yes, this is Yah,' he agreed, closing his fingers over her forearm. Yah was about his age, not especially glamorous and gave me a warm smile but said nothing. I asked the usual holiday questions and Rory explained that he had come to Ko Samui with ten men friends from Australia, but on the night they were leaving he had met Yah. That was nearly ten weeks ago. 'I would never have stayed if it wasn't for Yah,' he said, squeezing her arm again. He seemed proud of her, and also proud of this statement of his love.

'Aren't relationships like this compromised from the very beginning?' I asked him.

'Well, yes,' he agreed quickly, nodding. 'You do have to compromise, obviously. I mean, I have to come to terms with...you know, overlook her past. And now I'm going to speak very quickly, so she won't understand what I'm saying to you. There is the intellectual side, that's of course a disappointment, maybe a problem, and I have to overlook that, so that's another compromise.'

'I'm sorry, that's not quite what I meant. Isn't a relationship like this fundamentally corrupted?'

'Well,' he considered, 'I expect it raises your hackles as a Western woman. I feel uncomfortable with Western women now, I do sense their disapproval.'

'And how does that make you feel?

'It makes me think...' He paused, and pulled a series of weary, injured, irritated faces. 'It makes me think: Why? You see, I care about this lady a lot. I care about her. A lot.' He took her hand and stroked it. Yah was wearing a pleasant, blank smile, but facing away from the table. Rory talked as though she wasn't there. He seemed to be enjoying the conversation, measuring his opinions and pausing to admire the sound of each one as it came out. I asked if he would ever have expected to find himself in this situation.

'God no! Never! I would never have condoned it. I mean, I don't condone it. But when you travel, you know, you have to adapt, you have to examine your ideas, you know? And I think, well, if it makes a man happy for a few weeks, well then...'

'Well then, what?'

'Well then, that's a good thing, isn't it? And you know what? A lot of the ugliest men here, it turns out they're the nicest men. The really fat, ugly men, they treat their girl so well, they just want to be good to her.' I asked if he thought Yah would be with him if she was Australian.

'Oh, if she was Australian I would have left her weeks ago!'

'No, you misunderstand me. I mean, would she still choose to be with you if she was an Australian?'

'Ah. Oh, well... That's a tough one, I don't know.' He thought. 'You know, she could walk away whenever she wanted. She's as free as I am.'

'You believe all that?'

'Oh yeah. Y'see, I'd take a good argument over a pretty face any day. I want a wife, not a maid.' Rory said he was going back to Australia in two weeks' time. I asked if he was taking Yah with him. He said there were no plans for that as yet.

When we left, he said he hoped that we'd see each other again, and I think he meant it, for he was pleased with his performance and would have liked another chance to make his case. I found his presence disproportionately upsetting and avoided him, which was surprisingly easy to do in Chaweng. In spite—or perhaps because—of the town's boundless sexual licence, visitors seemed to need rituals, and one of these was a tendency to single out a particular bar and make it their local. I had met Rory in his local, and we never went back.

Paul and I had a local, too. Each night we would drop in at a tiny bamboo bar hidden down a mud track. It had just one bar girl, seldom any customers, and a young Swedish barman called Stefan, who was both boyishly sweet and fluent in all Chaweng's delusions. If the bar girl wanted to have sex for money, he said, it was nothing to do with him. 'I just want her to eat and be happy. I don't want to feel like a pimp.' When the girl did disappear with a man one night, though, he blustered and pretended not to know where they'd gone. He said the girls in Chaweng were treated wonderfully, but he was embarrassed when we asked if they were paid anything if no customers came in. 'That's not my side of the business.' The only time it seemed to count as prostitution for Stefan was the night a pair of particularly gross men, all paws and wet lips, took turns mauling the girl at the bar. 'That makes me so angry,' he shuddered. 'Urgh, they're so *big*.'

The girl in Stefan's bar had a buck-toothed smile that was too boisterous to be sexy and podgy legs dimpled like a baby's. Her walk was a playful waddle, more like a puppy's than a prostitute's. She beamed at us and chattered away to us every night, and because she looked so ungainly, so artless, we couldn't help ourselves. We began to believe she genuinely liked us.

'The girls, you know,' Stefan said quietly, in a rare lapse into honesty. 'They are not so nice. They really think about money, you know?' He meant it to be derogatory, but it was the only genuine compliment we ever heard the girls paid.

The night we arrived in Chaweng, it began to rain, and by dawn everywhere was knee-deep in water. Quite amused by the mess, we went out and bought raincoats—bright pink sheets of plastic with a hole in the middle for your head—and I was delighted by my new outfit, but would have been less so had I known it would be weeks before I could take it off. In the evenings the rain eased to a drizzle, but the deluge returned each morning and the town was rapidly reduced to a bog of rubbish and mud. For much of the time the electricity was down, so there were no showers or fans, and beneath our pink plastic we began to smell. This was unpleasant, but unimportant, because the whole strip stank. Miles of empty sand stretched out not twenty yards away, but we all stuck to the same septic gutter of concrete.

Tourists would start the day in the restaurants, where breakfast blurred into lunch, and movies were shown back to back. Diners tended to pick at their food, but stared intently at the television screen; violence was the staple theme. Afterwards, they drifted into shops and bought fake Nike trainers and fake Gucci belts, or they would start drinking again. The only reason why anyone was here— more than sunshine, more than bar girls, even—was that life on Ko Samui was cheap.

A man we met in a bar had calculated that his rent was 2.25 pence a night. His body was soldered on to a bar stool, but he swivelled round as soon as he heard Paul's Glasgow accent and introduced himself as Lenny from Falkirk. He was with five friends. 'This is my gang.' Lenny ran a pub in Spain called the Rovers' Return, and his friends were all landlords. Every winter they spent two or three months in Ko Samui while their Spanish pubs were closed. Most of them were staying in the bungalows near ours, though one was staying in the more expensive bungalows further up the beach. Lenny looked embarrassed. 'Wife's five months pregnant, you see.' We ran into Lenny and his gang every day, and the encounter always opened with a brief report of how much each of them had drunk the previous night. It was like calling a class register. They never seemed to get over how cheap the beer was, although they were knocked sideways one afternoon by a rumour that it was cheaper in Manila.

Besides cheap beer there was also Thailand's pharmaceutical free-for-all. Ko Samui's chemist's shops are as famous as Amsterdam's coffee shops in certain circles, and inspire the same sort of guzzling excitement. Sean took us to his favourite shop. The queue stretched to the door and a woman in a white coat was spooning pills out of large jars into plastic bags beneath a blackboard advertising VALIUM, VIAGRA, PROZAC, THE PILL, like a pub menu. A man in front of us asked about amphetamine pills and she frowned, said they were banned, then took a scoop of capsules out of a jar under the counter and slipped them into a bag with a wink. He pointed to some purple sleeping pills. 'Very good,' she nodded. 'When you wake up, there is nothing left in your brain.'

Sean's 'one hit' sale had been forgotten in the fun of handing out free Es to bar girls and his stock of pills was dwindling fast. There was something touching about his willingness to believe everything the girls told him. 'They'd never had an E before they met me!' he boomed with pride. We passed his local one afternoon and saw him leaning over, kissing a tiny girl who lay slumped on a chair. Her matchstick arm stuck out at an unnatural angle, like the limb of a dead child protruding from the scene of an accident.

The Full Moon rave was still almost a fortnight away, but we had lost the heart to wait any longer on Ko Samui, and so we sailed to Ko Pha-Ngan. Bar owners there had come up with an enterprising invention, the Half Moon party, thereby licensing themselves to hold three raves a month instead of one. Party-goers had proved relaxed about the finer points of lunar ritual, and around 10,000 flooded into the island every time. The next was due in a few days.

The ferry left from a dock near Chaweng. During the night the rain had finally ended and we found the upper deck jammed tight with backpackers fresh in from Bangkok and heading straight to Ko Pha-Ngan. A couple standing along the rail from us cracked Essex-girl-style jokes about Ko Samui, tossing fag ends into the water and lamenting the ruin of the island we were leaving behind. Most people said nothing at all, but put on sunglasses and did crosswords, or lay down to sleep. Even when the mountains and white sands of Ko Pha-Ngan came into view, mockingly beautiful, like an old Bounty Bar advert, nobody seemed to notice. Sunglasses and Walkmans stayed on as we docked in a shimmering sandy cove, and rucksacks were set down in silence on the jetty. Then along bounced a dozen or so pickup trucks; the drivers jumped out, called 'Taxi!', and everyone came to life.

'A hundred baht?' This was £1.50. 'Each? For ten of us?' Young men who five minutes earlier had been fast asleep swarmed around the drivers, waving their bronzed arms about in a pantomime of disgust. Rucksacks were thrown on to a truck, then snatched back when the driver refused to lower his price. 'Ten times a hundred—that makes a thousand baht!' a young Israeli screamed. He was tall and sinewy, wrapped in a kaftan, and the muscles in his neck stood taut with rage. He bent right down into the driver's face. 'A thousand baht! That's a lot of money for you.'

We decided to walk. The track to the main town of Had Rin was lined with single-storey shacks; some were bars, but most were either flip-flop shops or Internet cafes or both. MOSQUITO NET, read a sign outside one store, then: FAST SCREEN, SEVENTEEN-INCH, NON-RADIATION. There was no traffic or tarmac or bar girls, just a peaceful simplicity, but when we reached Had Rin we were still unprepared for the great sweep of beach facing us. It was long and creamy, framed by pearly boulders and turquoise surf, a cliché of tropical perfection. Pretty wooden huts on stilts were built into the cliff above us, and as we stood and stared, a man called down from the steps of one.

'You've got to be here, right. It'll go off here for sure. Best beach party in the world. Gotta be here. Unless you go to Goa, mind—you could be there, it'll go off in Goa too. But it goes off here all right, goes off every night.' He tipped a bottle of beer in welcome, and his friends waved hello. 'M'name's Neesy, we're from New Zealand.

Between us we've got fourteen years' travelling experience, and forty-three years' drinking experience. I think that's enough.' His friends nodded. 'Yep, hard core. But we're still working on it, for sure.'

Neesy was hard core all right. His nose was so badly burned that it looked like a crusty purple scab hanging on to his face. We would see him sauntering up and down the beach every day, commanding awe among more junior travellers, although also a little secret alarm. They would gaze in admiration as he passed, then hiss, 'Christ, did you see his nose?' when he was gone.

Backpackers on Ko Pha-Ngan looked nothing like the tourists on Ko Samui. At first glance, though, they did all look like each other. Everyone looked good, in the way young people do when they have lost a stone and grown used to wearing hardly any clothes. They were scuffed with bites and bruises, but these imperfections were all part of the look and so didn't really stand out. The Italians had good skin and wild hair, the Dutch had tattoos, and Americans came in rather serious, thirty-something couples, or as galumphing college boys, but this was as much as we noticed at first. To the naked eye, the Ko Pha-Ngan dress code appeared to be entirely relaxed.

It took a day or so to grasp the full hierarchy of style rules. A sensible Netherlands sandal was unsexy, but an obviously sexy shoe was out of the question, so anything involving straps or heels was unwise. A flip-flop worked best, implying frugality as well as beach bum/mountain goat agility. It was also important to have a tan deep enough to suggest you took being a backpacker seriously. The correct positioning of the knot in one's sarong was evidently a fraught issue; we watched one girl discreetly tie and re-tie hers using the reflection of a window for fifteen minutes. Bikinis were strictly of the stringy sort, thongs being too *Baywatch*, and underwired cups too C&A, and ethnic jewellery was essential, although too much betrayed amateurish enthusiasm. Combat shorts were all right for boys, if worn topless with a good tan, and the classier girl traveller rolled the waistband of her skirt down into a hipster. Here and there you would spy pale-skinned boys who had been thoughtless enough to come to Thailand wearing long trousers and Ben Sherman shirts. They stood about awkwardly, studying everyone else's outfits with dismay.

Friendliness was taken for inexperience, and considered shamefully gauche. It was safer to send emails than risk making conversation with each other, and this is what people spent a great deal of their time doing. The Internet cafes were so crowded that it was easy to spy on people's mail, and this revealed as much as anything we accomplished face to face. A high percentage of all emails began with 'Subject: Hangover', and a surprising number of those written by men gave rather arch and worldly accounts of the Bangkok sex industry. Middle-class boys composed wry emails to their fathers ('went to see women perform interesting acts with ping-pong balls'), and sauce to their mothers ('was offered sex for two hundred baht!!!'), followed by equally breezy but more graphic accounts to their friends of what happened when they accepted.

Few male backpackers had made it through Bangkok without paying to watch women eject ping-pong balls from their vaginas. Most were young men who would not visit a stripper or a prostitute at home, let alone tell their parents if they did, and yet Patpong was just part of the global itinerary, a morally neutral must-see. But there were no emails about the Thai tradition of eating dog, nor any other adventure in cultural relativism. Just a lot of emails about bargain sex.

Backpackers didn't talk about this. Nor did they explore any other anomaly in their lifestyle. As far as we could gather, the social code imposed a strict embargo on any discussion that could be considered controversial; what hippies would once have called 'heavy' was now discredited as inappropriate and girls in particular made quite a performance out of rolling their eyes at the first sign of trouble. Boys liked to boast about how little they knew of what was going on in the world, for to be caught knowing what was in the news was worse than tying your sarong the wrong way. Instead the favourite, if not the only conversation would always begin in the same way. 'Such and such a place,' someone would volunteer, 'is supposed to be *really* cheap.' And then everybody would sit up and listen.

Mountain Sea Bungalows were supposed to be really cheap. It was our first day on Ko Pha-Ngan and we were in a bar discussing where to stay when a French girl offered this advice. At once, two tall English blondes were at her table firing questions—how cheap?

where? what were they like?—and shortly we were making our way to Mountain Sea together. We found the owner on the veranda, being shouted at by a beautiful Italian about her bill. 'Look around us! Look at where we are!' The Italian girl's arm swept across the bay and the beach, and she stamped her foot. 'Look at all this—and we are talking about money!' The problem seemed to be that Mountain Sea had put up its rate by a few baht because of the Half Moon party. As backpackers outnumbered beds on the island, this was standard practice among the guest houses each time there was a party. Paul and I took a room. The two girls from London refused, 'on principle', and shared a supportive cigarette with the Italian. We agreed to look after their bags while they went to look elsewhere.

Each time they returned, they had bad news about another hotel hiking its prices by thirty pence a night. 'It's disgusting,' they said. 'They shouldn't be allowed to get away with it.'

Kate and Suzie were law graduates from the Home Counties, halfway round the world, and indignation seemed to be the theme of their tour. Time and again, Kate said, they'd arrived in a new place only to discover that the prices were way higher than anything they had been told to expect. Suzie wished they had gone straight to India now. Thais were just too greedy. Thailand was finished, she said. Ruined.

They ended up sleeping on our floor. During the day they dozed on the beach, practised their new hobby of juggling, or did sums in the flyleaves of their paperbacks to calculate how much they had spent. Their world tour was going to take them twelve months, but most of this time, it seemed, was going to be spent trying to save money, a pursuit they endowed with moral significance. 'Don't buy that there!' Suzie would chide strangers in shops. 'They're selling it for ten baht less over there.' She and Kate liked to show off their concave midriffs, not out of conventional vanity but as a boast of how little they'd managed to spend on food. They would sit up until the early hours trading tips with other backpackers on where in the world one could best avoid spending money.

Kate and Suzie expected to become lawyers. In the meantime, however, having volunteered to survive on eight pounds a day, they chose to think of themselves as poor people. 'Look, I've only got eight pounds a day, all right?' Suzie would remind anyone whom she felt was failing to make every possible concession to her self-imposed poverty. Thais should give her a break, she thought, and she was forever losing her temper with another shopkeeper who didn't seem to understand that she was on a budget. 'Fucking rip-off merchants,' she would hiss to Kate, handing over her coins with a scowl.

It was true that eight pounds, or 500 baht, was not a lot to get by on in Thailand. A beer cost sixty baht, a meal maybe 200, and our bungalow in Chaweng had been 450 baht a night. But if Kate and Suzie were facing a measure of austerity, it was nothing to what the Thais had suffered after the crash of 1997. Since that summer, when the baht lost almost half its value and the economy practically collapsed, unemployment had more than doubled and inflation was running at seven per cent. For a time this had represented a jackpot for backpackers, the devalued baht making Thailand a tropical bargain to rival even Goa. Word had spread that one could live like a king on 200 baht a day. Happily for Thailand, this was no longer true, but backpackers seemed to treat this development like a broken promise. Most of them regarded the tentative recovery with outright indignation, and attributed the price rises to downright greed.

I suggested to Suzie that if she had come away for less time, she could have had a bigger budget and would not have had to spend her journey thinking about money. 'But you have to have a year,' she corrected me, looking confused. 'I mean, that's what you get, isn't it?' To Suzie, the year out was the constitutional right of all young professionals, and it was the duty of the Third World to keep her within her budget.

After a couple of days we left our room to the two of them and travelled up the coast, to a guest house tucked away in the jungle where, it had been suggested, we might find the true spirit of Thailand. The Sanctuary styled itself as a retreat for travellers who had come to experience a culture rather than a discount economy. It was a picturesque cluster of wooden platforms on stilts built into the cliffs of a deserted cove; low tables and cushions and hammocks were dotted about, ethnic trance music played softly in the background, and the waves lapped below. A board behind the curved stone bar was reserved for a THOUGHT FOR THE DAY. When we arrived, the thought was: ONCE YOU REALIZE GOD KNOWS EVERYTHING, YOU ARE TRULY FREE. Another sign suggested: TRY TO REALIZE YOU ARE A DIVINE TRAVELLER. YOU ARE ONLY HERE FOR A LITTLE WHILE, THEN DEPART FOR A DISSIMILAR AND FASCINATING WORLD.

The woman in charge spoke in a low, dreamy voice, and appeared to float rather than walk, as though the gravity had been turned down wherever she went. Most of the guests were trying to copy her, and greeted our arrival with slow-motion nods of the head and whispered half-smiles. One of them led us to the library, a corner of bookshelves lodged into the rocks, and encouraged us to try a book about the mystical significance of birthdays, but by this point we were ravenous, having not liked to be caught eating anything in Had Rin, so we declined the book and ordered a mountain of food. When we had finished eating, we had to say 'Paul and Decca' to the waitress. No money changed hands until it was time to check out, and our tab was filed under our names instead of our room number. 'When you stay at the Sanctuary,' they would remind any guest who needed it spelled out, 'you are not a number, you are an indiv...' and so on.

It was a relief to go whole days without hearing anybody mention money. It was prudent of the owners to operate such a system, though, as their prices were at least double the going rate everywhere else. The Sanctuary belonged to an Irishman, and the staff in charge were all Westerners. They sold the Sanctuary as an experience of pure Thailand, yet were alone among Thai businesses in having contrived not only to overcharge backpackers, but to get them to pay without complaining.

Most of the guests were British. They worked in the arts or media, liked yoga and boiled rice, and tied their sarongs in inventively new twists. Most were subtly possessive about the Sanctuary. They sighed about 'other' backpackers, the *Lonely Planet* hordes in Had Rin who showed no respect for Thailand, and in an interesting inversion of tradition, they took pride in paying Sanctuary prices. It was as though by spending more rather than less, they hoped to prove their authenticity as travellers.

In the next bay along lived a Thai housewife in a Robinson Crusoe-style shack. She spoke no English, but would rustle up an omelette for thirty baht—a fraction of the price charged at the

Sanctuary—but its guests seldom climbed the headland to eat her food. Like all the travellers we met, they spoke not a word of Thai, so they preferred to swing in hammocks at the Sanctuary, enthusing among themselves and the staff about the beauty of 'real' Thailand. One man was worried when he saw Paul taking photographs. 'Don't say the name of the beach,' he murmured confidentially. 'Just say, "a beach".'

The Half Moon party took place the following night. We caught a small boat down the coast to Had Rin with two Australian nurses who were taking the night off from their meditation studies at the Sanctuary. They urged us to try it, calling it 'cosmic'. Arriving at Had Rin, the boat man asked for a hundred baht each. 'A hundred baht?' shouted one of them. 'It's a fifty-baht ride! Right, take us back, you wanker, and we'll get a fifty-baht ride.' The other nurse stood over him and wagged a finger, repeating: '*Bad* business. *Bad* business,' in a voice you might use to talk to a dog. 'Nice meeting ya. Have a great party!' she called to us as we climbed ashore, then turned back to the man. '*Bad* business.'

And so here at last was the famous Ko Pha-Ngan party. The beach had been re-fashioned into a late-Eighties warehouse party, with fairy lights glowing in the cliffs, and strobes raking the beach, catching luminous crescent moons of silk staked along the sand. The effect was spooky, and unexpectedly pretty—although perhaps not as unexpected as the lengths everyone had gone to to dress up for the occasion. As if by secret pre-arrangement, they had come as ravers circa 1988. Girls wore spray-tight trousers in amusingly lurid patterns, boys came as ironic tramps in woolly hats, and both wore gigantic trainers and strode up and down in tight little groups, faces hardened by expectation. Those wearing the wrong outfit hovered on the edges, gratifying the others with their abject inferiority.

People drank beer, and took speed and magic mushrooms, and apart from the unlucky few whose hallucinogens made them stand by themselves and scowl at the sand, they danced. I recognized the dance from raves a decade ago; it looked like a small child's impersonation of a mentally handicapped person, and it skidded around in a circle, incoherent and demented. Round and round everyone spun, all the way down the beach, most narrowly managing to miss the beat, and some apparently dancing to a different record altogether. As the night wore on the dancing thinned, and thousands of people lay back in the sand on their elbows, smoking cigarettes and gazing about them in wonder. 'Wicked,' they nodded, grinning at each other. 'Wicked.'

Drifting from one cluster to the next, I realized the conversations were also familiar from old raves, when everyone used to laugh about discos and girls who wore make-up. Here, it was Ko Samui they were mocking—tatty, tarty Ko Samui, lavishly scorned with the same lazy pleasure all the way along the beach. One group was unable to let the matter go, and as the night wore on its members became worked up about the need to protect Ko Pha-Ngan from the vulgar tribe over the water. As custodians of paradise, everyone agreed, they had a duty to keep out the beer bellies and credit cards.

In the dark I lay and listened. I was reminded of Sean and his friends on Ko Samui, and after a while I found I couldn't see any difference between them and the backpackers, except that Sean's lot paid up for their pleasures without complaining. As the temperature dropped before dawn, and they kept on talking, I realized I couldn't see any difference between the backpackers and us, either. I had taken it for granted that the Thais were happier to have Paul and me there, rather than the other tourists, because we weren't rude. But the backpackers assumed that prostitutes preferred sleeping with them rather than with men like Sean because they weren't ugly, and I had thought them contemptible for flattering themselves about it.

All any of us had done in Thailand was buy things. Travelling like this is a euphemism for shopping, an endless spree, and whether we were buying breakfast or sex, we were doing it primarily because it was cheap. Paul and I had thought it funny and slightly tragic that the couple in the hotel bar in Bangkok had come all this way for a fake handbag, believing themselves to be on an exotic adventure. It hadn't occurred to us that we might be the same.

And if we were, then the great debate about who was to blame for spoiling Thailand was meaningless. Everyone who came to Thailand to spend foreign earnings on fun was defined by the gap between their wealth and Thailand's poverty. Despite the backpackers' belief in their own poverty, what they actually take from Thailand is the experience of being immensely rich. They behave in the same careless, bored and discontented way as rich people anywhere, with no purpose but their own amusement. Guarding their money like millionaires, they greet every Thai with suspicion, and mix only with their own. It is a cruel irony for those who set off imagining they will find themselves by travelling, and find instead their identities are reduced to the sum of their traveller's cheques.

Long-haul travel on this scale is scarcely a generation old. It began in the Seventies, in overland lorries to Kathmandu, and it was only in the Eighties that around-the-world tickets became common-place. The expression 'gap year' wasn't heard outside public schools until the Nineties. Yet already it is accepted without question that a long stint away from home, in somewhere like Thailand, is an essential and improving experience. And so here we all were on a beach, observing the convention, impersonating the time of our lives.

The sun rose slowly over a rubbish tip of empty bottles and debris and raddled dancers. Their basic move had evolved into a hunched stomp by now, like the posture of an elderly woman who has just heard a mugger coming up behind her, and their eyes were pink and bloodshot. Men were standing knee-deep in the ocean, peeing. A scattering of girls lay sobbing on the sand, wretched with exhaustion now the drugs had worn off, and at the far end of the beach taxi drivers were herding the unsteady into pickup trucks. We threaded our way through the casualties and boarded one, but just as we were pulling away, a skinny young man stumbled up and threw himself in over the tailgate, face first.

'I just wanna wind them up, like,' he slurred at our feet, in a thick Welsh accent. 'Say I won't pay more than thirty baht.'

The driver said quietly that the fare was sixty baht. The Welshman took a swig from a bottle of whisky, levered himself on to his elbows, and told him to fuck off. A laugh and cheer went up in the truck—and there was a noisy commotion, then we were all out of the truck, and then we were all in again, minus the Welshman, and agreeing to pay the fare. But by now the driver wanted it in advance, and as we were paying the Welshman came flying in again, head first, crash-landing between our legs with the whisky bottle held safely aloft in an outstretched hand. Calmly, the driver leaned in again, and asked for the fare.

'Fuck off,' spat the Welshman.

'Just pay him,' I pleaded.

'No, I like to wind them up.'

'Please, pay him the fare.'

'Shut up, it's a laugh.'

'For Christ's sake, *pay him!*' I screamed. He blinked, startled, and Paul's hand closed on my arm as I made to fly at him. The other passengers stared at me in amazement, and the two women on board slid supportive hands on to the Welshman's shoulder. Still the driver waited for his fare. At the front, two Swedish skinheads lost their tempers.

'Drive the car! Drive the car!' they roared in unison at the driver. Their hairless pink faces were twisted with fury, and they were stamping their feet on the floor. *'Fuck-ing drive the fuck-ing car! Drive! The! Car!'* Then everyone was shouting at the driver, and in the uproar someone paid for the Welshman, and suddenly we were off, bumping along a dusty track through the jungle in the raw morning sunshine. For a few minutes the surprise of being under way silenced us all, and I realized that I was shaking.

The bundle at our feet stirred. The Welshman pulled himself upright, gazed around, rubbed his eyes, took another swig, and offered the bottle around. 'It's only a laugh, stupid,' he grinned, catching sight of my expression. 'It's only a laugh. They're thieving bastards anyway.'

'How much do you earn?'

'Fifteen hundred pounds a month. So what?'

'There's not one person in this vehicle who earns as little as the man driving it. Why do you think you can treat him like that?'

'I don't want to be lectured. I'm travelling.'

'That doesn't give you a licence to act like a cunt.'

A shock jolted around the truck, and I felt hostile eyes settle on me. The two girls stroked the Welshman's neck, and a man at the back shook his head slowly and let out a low whistle. The skinhead boys squared their shoulders and then one of them said, 'I think you'd better mind your manners, young lady, don't you? There's no need to be rude.'   □

I HEARD IT THROUGH THE GRAPEVINE
James Campbell

James Baldwin, London 1964

I Heard It Through the Grapevine

At the turn of 1962–3, James Baldwin was regarded as a writer with the power of healing. He spoke across chasms: male–female, father–son, straight–queer; most of all, Baldwin seemed capable of locating the hurt good white Americans felt at being separated, by crimes too ancient and convoluted to contemplate, from their black countrymen—neighbours, schoolfriends, wet nurses, lovers, even children. The passage most often quoted from Baldwin's work is the one which occurs near the end of 'Down at the Cross', the essay which forms the larger part of *The Fire Next Time*. It spread over eighty-five pages of the *New Yorker* in November 1962:

> If we—and now I mean the relatively conscious whites and the relatively conscious blacks, who must, like lovers, insist on, or create, the consciousness of the others—do not falter in our duty now, we may be able, handful that we are, to end the racial nightmare and achieve our country...

And, he added, 'change the history of the world'. The rhetorical flourish was unnecessary, though it was becoming a common feature of his style, as the urgency of his message increased. 'Change' was Baldwin's text. He grew up in Harlem tenements in the 1920s and 30s literally praying for change, and embraced it in the storefront churches which still dot uptown New York streets today. At the age of fourteen, Baldwin became a Young Minister in the Baptist church, urging Harlem denizens to change their ways. *The Fire Next Time* was his secular sermon, addressed mainly to whites, but its moral ardour was equal to that of the boy preacher: 'Change, or your sin will find you out.' Baldwin had long since lost his Christian faith, but not his conviction that the soul hovered dangerously between redemption and damnation, depending on a mere human action to determine its fate.

The Fire Next Time was published as a book in January 1963. By June, it had entered a tenth printing. Everything changed for Baldwin that year. Two other books—the novel, *Another Country*, and a collection of essays, *Nobody Knows My Name*—were already best-sellers. In May, *Time* magazine paid tribute to his influence by putting his face on the cover, which led in turn to a personal invitation from the Attorney General, Robert Kennedy, to hold a meeting to address the widening chaos in the South. Bombs were exploding in black leaders' houses, churches were being set on fire, civil rights workers and all who followed them walked in constant fear for their lives. When Martin Luther King led the March on Washington in August, Baldwin fell in behind the leader, expecting to be among the key speakers (we will return to the reasons why he was not). A writer known for his delicate examinations of private themes had suddenly become a public figure, or, to use the term he disliked so much, a 'spokesman'.

Something else happened to Baldwin that year. He lost his faith for a second time; a humanist faith. The moment can be traced back to the meeting with RFK, which took place in the Attorney General's New York office on May 24. Baldwin brought along a troupe of friends, colleagues and showbusiness personalities—Harry Belafonte, Lena Horne and the playwright Lorraine Hansberry were among those present—and a young man from the Deep South who had been badly beaten during the Freedom Rides of 1961, the efforts to integrate Southern waiting rooms and lunch counters by travelling in special buses from town to town. To Baldwin, Jerome Smith's broken bones gave him a greater authority than anyone else in the room. During the increasingly heated exchanges, Smith waved a finger in the Attorney General's face and declared that he would never fight to defend his country, since his country had noticeably failed to defend him (in trying to use the same waiting rooms as whites, the Freedom Riders were only acting within their constitutional rights). According to eyewitness accounts, Kennedy recoiled visibly at this. He was more shocked by it than by anything else said during the meeting. Baldwin was shocked, too, but for a different reason.

Smith's bleak comment, and that made to him by another young black man at the same time, 'I got no country, I got no flag,' would chime in Baldwin's mind a few days after the encounter with Kennedy, when he announced to a reporter from the *New York Times* that '22 million black people cannot be negotiated with any more'. He added: 'There is no possibility of a bargain whatsoever.' It chimed again, some months later, when he accused the Kennedy administration and the FBI of a 'lack of action' following the bombing of a church in Birmingham, Alabama, in which four little black girls were killed. And again, when he told a rally in Washington, DC that he knew of 'many people, even members of my own family, who would think nothing of picking up arms tomorrow'.

These remarks and many others, more despairing than belligerent, were copied down, typed up on headed notepaper, and logged in Baldwin's new FBI file. A card marked 'BALDWIN, JAMES ARTHUR, 1924– , NEGRO, MALE...' had been filled out in 1960, after Baldwin signed a petition organized by the pro-Castro Fair Play for Cuba Committee. Now, following the affront to Robert Kennedy, his status was to be upgraded. Four days after the meeting, on May 28, Clyde Tolson, Associate Director to J. Edgar Hoover, circulated a newspaper report of the meeting among FBI colleagues at Washington headquarters, together with the query: 'What do our files show about James Baldwin?' The following day, Crime Records division requested 'a check of the New York indices for any information [on Baldwin], particularly of a derogatory nature'. The summary was required 'for dissemination to the Attorney General'. Although Baldwin continued to regard the Attorney General as an ally, Kennedy had ordered FBI reports on several of those who had humiliated him in his own office, and authorized a wiretap to be installed on the telephone of at least one, Clarence Jones, a lawyer who worked for Martin Luther King.

A forty-five-page report on Baldwin was drawn up, the basis of a dossier which would soon grow to over a thousand pages. The report included details of Baldwin's education, military status, residences past and present, criminal record ('subject was arrested on September 3, 1954, on a charge of disorderly conduct'), publication history, bank records, and every other detail of his behaviour and opinions that could be unearthed. His name was placed on the Security Index, the list of 'dangerous individuals' who posed 'a threat to national security', who would be rounded up first in a state of emergency. A link was made, via sinuous logic, to the Communist Party: 'In 1961 he sponsored a news release from the Carl Braden Clemency Appeal Committee distributed by the Southern Conference Educational Fund.' Braden had been 'identified as CP member' and the Fund was 'the successor to the Southern Conference for Human Welfare cited as a Communist front by the House Committee on Un-American Activities'. Two years on, Baldwin would quite likely have been unable to remember the 'news release'—a petition bearing his signature, among many others—and almost certainly would never have heard of the defunct Southern Conference for Human Welfare, allegedly a 'communist front'. But from now on his card would always be marked COMMUNIST, whereas, in fact, he had no formal affiliation to any political organization, not even among civil rights groups. In keeping with the spirit of Baldwin's sudden visibility in the news media, the FBI made no distinction between private and public affairs.

After Baldwin's death, in November 1987, I began to write a book about him. In the course of my research, I applied for access to his FBI file, under the United States Freedom of Information Act (FOIA). Baldwin often referred to his 'friendly file', sometimes in my presence, and was certain that, on more than one occasion, his telephone had been bugged. Friends and relatives would allude to the same thing, and, amid the natural outrage, you could sense the feeling of continuing importance it induced. Late in life, Baldwin's literary reputation had taken a drastic fall, and his public image shrank with it; but he retained the belief that he was being badgered by government agencies. The most recent persecutor was the Internal Revenue Service. Baldwin told me that he intended to arrange his tax affairs in the neatest possible order, 'And then I'm going to sue them.' I have the clearest mental picture of the fury in his face—an anger deeper than resentment at fiscal bullying could explain. 'I got no country, I got no flag,' the reproach that triggered an internal change in 1963, had become his own bitterly unwelcome banner.

In cases where the subject is no longer living, the procedure for requesting an FBI file is simple: 'May 10, 1988. Dear Sir/Madam, I request access to the FBI file on James Baldwin, under the Freedom of Information Act.' An acknowledgement that there existed 'investigative files responsive to your request', together with a plea for patience, came back within two weeks. I was patient. Eighteen months later, all I had received on Baldwin was a few documents in which his name was mentioned in passing; whole paragraphs, even entire pages (except the words 'JAMES BALDWIN', peeping through the black veil), had been deleted according to 'subsections of Title 5, United States Code, Section 552'. Mostly, these 'exemptions' concern the protection of the privacy of informants, or of other people mentioned, including friends of the subject. Or else they refer to 'national security'. So wide-ranging were the exemptions that the agents responsible for reviewing the documents believed they were entitled to delete every item of information, together with its context, concerning even an unwitting informant, or any person who is not dead (or whose death has not come to the attention of the FBI) or who has not specifically waived the right to privacy. 'National security', it hardly needs saying, is an elastic term.

On the advice of an experienced user of the Freedom of Information Act, I wrote to a lawyer in Washington, James Lesar, who, it was promised, could speed up the process of review. A friendly, overworked attorney in private practice who single-handedly puts to death the caricature of the avaricious American lawyer, Lesar advised that the only way to obtain substantial 'disclosure'—a word he uses often—without a further long wait, was to file suit against the FBI. This sounded alarming to me, but it was action Lesar was used to taking, and so, after settling on a fixed fee, we duly went to court on the grounds that an author was being hindered in his pursuit of an honest living.

Soon afterwards, a large box thumped on to my doorstep. It contained 1,000 pages, including many duplications and useless copies of index cards, from the records that FBI HQ in Washington, and field offices in New York, Los Angeles and San Francisco, had compiled on Baldwin. Smaller batches of records came from the CIA, and from Army and Air Force intelligence services. The huge black squares of 'exemptions' were everywhere; in places a form had been interleaved, stating that a number of pages had been withheld.

Many documents were accessible, however, even when they had not evaded the dead hand of the censor; enough for me to see that Baldwin's political engagement had been answered, in proportion, by secret and continuous surveillance, in New York, Hollywood and the American South, in Istanbul, Rome and elsewhere. Spies had gathered information from unwitting neighbours and relatives, either by telephone or in person. Among them were FBI agents 'posing as a newspaper reporter', 'posing as a publisher', 'using the pretext of being a foreign auto sales representative', 'posing as a college student', 'on the pretext of being an American Express representative', and so on. Agents would attend any meeting at which Baldwin was advertised as a speaker, and the organization which had invited him would be scrutinized for links to the Communist Party. Afterwards, a report would be written up of what had been seen or heard, and so a substantial 'investigative' file on James Baldwin, a 'person likely to pose a threat to the security of the United States', was compiled. I gleaned what I could from it and finished my book.

Lesar, however, has spent twenty years nipping at the heels of the investigative agencies in order to obtain greater disclosure. 'I get personally incensed every time I see stuff being withheld, where it has not been adequately explained to me why. I recognized at the outset that it would be bad practice to go score a quick victory, declare victory, and hang it up. The agencies would take advantage of that situation. They had to know and understand that I was going to be there as long as possible.' Lesar is a specialist on the assassination of John F. Kennedy in Dallas in 1963, and is president of the Assassination Archives and Research Center. We agreed that he would proceed with the case, in order to attempt to extract more information about the surveillance of Baldwin, and so began *James Campbell, plaintiff v. US Department of Justice, defendant*, a nine-year legal slog, which came to a head on December 29, 1998, at the Court of Appeals in Washington, the second most powerful court in the United States, with what Lesar calls a resounding decision. Although the case bears my name, the victory is Lesar's. The Appeal Court judges decided 3–0 in the plaintiff's favour, giving us victory on almost every front. Judge Judith Rogers, who delivered the forty-five-point Opinion of the Court, issued a series of stern rebukes to the FBI, over its past conduct and its present manipulation of the Freedom of Information Act. After the sitting, Lesar overheard a Bureau supervisor saying of Judge Rogers: 'She trashed us.' Baldwin would have been interested to know that; and to learn that Lesar counts *Campbell* among the most important decisions in all his years of FOIA litigation.

My acquaintance with Baldwin began in the late 1970s, when he
agreed to write an essay for the *New Edinburgh Review*, of which
I was then the editor. I would say that I was friendly with him in a
respectfully distant way—but it was impossible to be distant from
Baldwin once a friendship had begun. I stayed as a guest at his house
outside the village of St-Paul de Vence, near Nice, on several
occasions, and chaperoned him around London—with Baldwin, there
was always the role of Man Friday to be filled—and later on he
visited Edinburgh, where I interviewed him in front of a live audience
at the Festival. I was proud of our working relationship, and he,
sensing that I did not like to be counted among the hangers-on,
would introduce me to others, with an avuncular wink, as 'one of
my editors'.

The essay, which was ostensibly a review of a book about jazz,
was called 'Of the Sorrow Songs', echoing W. E. B. Du Bois's famous
chapter on Negro folk song in *The Souls of Black Folk*. Baldwin
improvised relentlessly in the course of the piece, dissecting his theme,
then restoring it, in a tone entirely his own:

> This music begins on the auction-block. Whoever is unable to face
> this...whoever pretends that the slave mother does not weep, until
> this hour, for her slaughtered son...can never pay the price for the
> *beat* which is the key to music, and the key to life.

Many baleful changes had occurred since his appeal to the
'relatively conscious' in *The Fire Next Time*. The reply, it seemed to
him, was like the crack of a repeating gun: in June 1963, Medgar
Evers of the National Association for the Advancement of Colored
People was shot outside his home in Jackson, Mississippi; two years
later, Malcolm X was killed in Harlem; then Martin Luther King in
Memphis in 1968. A new generation of young radicals emerged, and
some of them were killed too, in battles with the police or prison
officers.

The middle and later years of the 1960s were not prolific ones
for the writer. Between 1963 and 1973, Baldwin produced only one
novel, *Tell Me How Long the Train's Been Gone*, a sprawling first-
person tale, bedevilled by flashbacks, and bearing a more ponderous

racial burden than his previous work. To critics who asked if politics had edged out literature in his life, Baldwin would reply, with studied coolness, that he had been 'trying to write between assassinations'. In an 'Open Letter to My Sister, Angela Davis', in 1970, he indicated where the bright hopes of the early part of the decade had led: the day had come 'to render impassable with our bodies the corridor to the gas chamber. For, if they take you in the morning, they will be coming for us that night.' Another sermon for another time. When critics or journalists, or just well-meaning friends, asked, 'Gas chamber?', Baldwin stared back and repeated: 'Gas chamber.'

The murder of King, in particular, froze his heart. In an interview conducted two years after the assassination, Baldwin was asked about current projects. He replied that he was writing 'a long essay on the life and death of the civil rights movement'. Taken aback, the interviewer asked: 'It died?' 'Yes,' said Baldwin. 'It died with Martin... We've marched and petitioned for a decade, and now it's clear there's no point in marching or petitioning. And what happens I don't know, but when they killed Martin they killed that hope.'

By the time I first arrived at the old farmhouse on a hillside just beneath St-Paul de Vence, he had written and published his essay on the movement, but it was an incomplete, diary-style account (*No Name in the Street*, 1972), and the subject continued to preoccupy him. He was trying to get started on a 'triple biography' of Medgar Evers, Malcolm X and Martin Luther King, and he wore a watch with King's face on it, a portrait in cartoon colours of the martyr with head raised, mouth open, as if in mid-flow. King, though five years younger, was his mentor, and the watch strapped round Baldwin's wrist was a band of fidelity to King's crusade, which was, in essence, a biblical crusade: the deliverance from the land of bondage. Baldwin gave the impression of living every hour at the crook of optimism and despair. To spend a day in his company meant traversing his entire emotional territory. His mood determined the mood of every gathering at which he was present. Writing to his brother David in 1969, he characterized a self divided into three: a 'mad-man', determined to change the world; a 'fragile, gifted child'; and a 'superbly paranoiac intelligence'. All three were actively competing at all times.

My first sight of him was across the village square, on a Tuesday afternoon. At the conclusion of the long and sometimes comical sequence of telephone calls required to coax him into fulfilling his commission for the *New Edinburgh Review*, Baldwin had invited me to 'drop by', as he put it, 'if you ever happen to be down this way'. He probably issued many such invitations, but I took him at his word. During a sojourn in Paris, I rang to say I was thinking of dropping by. He said: 'I'd love that.' I offered to call again before boarding the train for Nice, but the suggestion was brushed aside. 'I look forward to meeting you,' he said in the smoky baritone which bobbed in and out of French and American intonations.

In spite of all that, he forgot that I was coming. 'Oh, baby,' he said, when I rang from outside the station in Nice, 'I wish you'd let me *know*.' But it was said without annoyance, and when I crossed the square in St-Paul, where men were playing boules, he raised the shades above his eyes, took my hand, and said: 'Are you him?' It is rare, Baldwin wrote about his first meeting with Martin Luther King in 1958, 'that one *likes* a world-famous man—by the time they become world famous they rarely like themselves'. Yet, he continued, in a phrase which I would apply to him, his hero was 'immediately and tremendously winning, there is really no other word for it'.

I stayed five days. Baldwin rose around noon. After his second coffee, he would move on to Johnnie Walker Black Label. The menu varied throughout the day, beer in the afternoon and wine with meals. At about one in the morning, he would cast a glance at the whisky bottle and say: 'I'm going to have a last drink and then go downstairs to do some work.' I would join him in that drink, and we would talk until four or five.

A moral force drove everything he said, even his witty, frequently self-effacing small talk. Every one of us was living on the Redeemer's account. 'People pay for what they do, and they pay for it very simply—by the lives they lead.' His huge, searching, vulnerable eyes shone their lights on every conversation. When his assistant, Bernard Hassell, a tough, likeable New Yorker, complained about some righteous hip type, who had called on Brother Baldwin a month before and left with a fistful of money which would never be repaid, Baldwin simply shrugged. Only the miscreant could suffer, in that transaction. It was up to him to foresee the desert to which his actions would lead him.

The piece he wrote for the *New Edinburgh Review* came out in the syncopated, 'blue' style which had become his mode, replacing the lovely logical elegance of his work from the years spanning 1953 to 1962, a decade which produced three novels, *Go Tell It on the Mountain*, *Giovanni's Room* and *Another Country*, and three books of essays, *Notes of a Native Son*, *Nobody Knows My Name* and *The Fire Next Time*; work which led to Baldwin being crowned, in Lionel Trilling's phrase, 'the monarch of the current literary jungle'. The triple biography, though, would never get written. Nor would a novel, *No Papers for Mohammed*, for which he signed a contract in the early 1970s. Somewhere at the base of my esteem, I was aware that a trauma had occurred to separate the writer I admired so strongly that I continued to read his books over and over, and the writer sitting opposite me. Baldwin flashed brilliant remarks across the table, and had immense generosity and humour, but he was less and less inclined to think in a dialectical manner. 'She is a victim, therefore she is my sister,' he said of Angela Davis. As a young writer, he had possessed natural gifts perhaps unequalled among his contemporaries; he had superb control over rhythm, phrasing, the structure of an argument and the poise proper to its resolution. But the years of harassment, culminating symbolically in the assassination of King, permanently affected his balance. 'Since Martin's death... something has altered in me,' he wrote in *No Name in the Street*, 'something has gone away.'

Two

The decision of the court meant that the FBI had to go back and review all files relating to Baldwin again, to reprocess them in line with the judges' directions. 'The record suggests that the FBI made an abstract attempt to identify possible public interests in disclosure and accorded these interests surprisingly little weight,' said Judge Rogers, in what Lesar regards as one of the most censorious public scoldings administered to the FBI by a legal figure. 'This attitude is troubling given the presumption of openness inherent in the Freedom of Information Act.' The adequacy of the Bureau's search for documents, she said, was insufficient. In the view of the Court, the FBI had resorted to the pesky exemptions—specifically those governing National Security (Exemption 1) and Law Enforcement (Exemption 7)—too zealously and too frequently. The present administration was reminded of 'the obvious historical value of documents describing the FBI's role [in the cold war and] in the civil rights movement'. The privacy of individuals deserved consideration, but ought to be balanced against historical interest, in a case in which the documents date back more than thirty years. The three judges of the Court of Appeals concluded that the FBI had treated 'the balancing process in the instant case as somewhat of an empty formality'. The following gives a taste of the Opinion (164 F 3d 20, DC Cir 1998):

> The Department [of Justice] has identified only two facts to establish that documents relating to James Baldwin were compiled for a law enforcement purpose. First, the FBI relies on a declaration from Special Agent Regina Supernau, in which she lists the names of the files containing withheld information. The relevant labels are: 'Interstate Transportation of Obscene Material', 'Security Matter—Communism', and 'Internal Security'. The fact that information is stored inside a folder with an official-sounding label is insufficient standing alone to uphold nondisclosure...
>
> Second, the Department relies on a statement in the declaration of Special Agent Debra Mack that 'the FBI investigation of James Baldwin was predicated upon the fact that established security sources of the FBI had indicated that James Baldwin was associating with persons and organizations which were believed to be a threat to the security of the United States'... The FBI appears to maintain that once it can justify its investigation of a person, all documents related to that person are exempt from FOIA, even if the documents were collected for a different reason.

And so it continues, 'issue after issue', as Lesar delightedly said to me. 'The rulings are not the only measure of the significance of the *Campbell* decision,' he added. 'Its tone and attitude will be extremely helpful to a host of FOIA requesters.' More than a year after the verdict, a new edition of Baldwin's file arrived on my doorstep, significantly augmented in comparison to the one I'd received almost ten years earlier. According to an enclosed letter from the Chief, FOIA Section, John M. Kelso, it included '108 pages released for the first time and 625 pages now released in full'. It was not crammed with sensational revelations, but it gave a more ample, detailed picture of the global surveillance to which Baldwin was subjected while attempting, as he would put it, to bear witness; or, more simply, while exercising his right to freedom of speech.

The wiretap placed on the telephone of Clarence Jones, King's lawyer, after the meeting with RFK, was to be the conduit for a great many conversations between Jones and others, including Baldwin, concerning the overall strategy of King's Southern Christian Leadership Conference (SCLC). No record has been released of a similar authorization for electronic surveillance of Baldwin, though many of his conversations were recorded via bugs on the telephones of others. He himself was certain that an attempt had been made to install a device, and complained to journalists—and to the FBI—that three days after the Kennedy meeting two men had turned up at his apartment on East 18th Street and tried to gain entry, only to be refused by the doorman. Hoover took swift action to deny this, in a letter to President Kennedy's special assistant, Kenneth O'Donnell:

> It should be noted that an allegation has been made that Agents of the New York Office had attempted to enter Baldwin's apartment on May 27, 1963, and the further allegation has been made that persons attending the conference [with RFK] had been interviewed by Agents following the conference. Both allegations are completely false... Baldwin has not been harassed in any way by agents of this Bureau.

The Assistant Attorney General, Burke Marshall, later admitted to a *New York Post* journalist, Fern Eckman, that the two men were FBI agents (though he denied that their purpose was to plant a bug). In any case, harassment by other means had begun. According to Natalie Robbins, author of *Alien Ink: The FBI's War on Freedom*

With Marlon Brando, August 28, 1963 (also Charlton Heston, left, and Harry Belafonte)   AP

of Expression (1992), 'For Hoover, those who were anti-FBI were as dangerous as those who were pro-Communist.' Baldwin's name was already linked to communist-front organizations—which, in Hoover's mind, might be a left-leaning body such as the National Lawyers Guild—but now attention focused on his attacks on Hoover himself. After the bombing of the church in Birmingham, he told a journalist: 'I blame Hoover.' An article in the *Washington Post* ended with a quotation from another interview: 'First of all...you've got to get rid of J. Edgar Hoover and the power that he wields. If you could get rid of [him]...there would be a great deal more hope.' There followed many more assaults on the integrity of the Director— Hoover was 'not a lawgiver [nor] a particularly profound student of human nature'—and they all passed through FBI memos to be incorporated into Baldwin's Security Index file, as proof that he posed a threat to national security.

An example of how persistent the FBI could be in tracking down statements unfavourable to the Director concerns the case of a television programme made by the US Information Agency (USIA) on August 28, 1963, the day of the March on Washington. Through the wiretap on Jones's phone, the FBI learned that Baldwin had made 'remarks regarding the FBI and Mr Hoover' while being filmed for the broadcast. 'The substance of his remarks...were "Part of the problem in the civil rights movement is J. Edgar Hoover".'

This section of the programme had been edited out before transmission. Still, Hoover wrote personally to the Director of the Office of Security at the USIA, Paul McNichol, to enquire about the situation. McNichol dutifully replied (October 11, 1963) that 'the portion of Mr Baldwin's remarks which were removed contained attacks on you and Senator James Eastland'. It was USIA policy, however, that 'if an individual is attacked by name, some answer to the attack must be included'. Since there was no answer, Baldwin's comments had been cut.

The Bureau would not leave it there. Domestic Intelligence division contacted McNichol and demanded a verbatim account of Baldwin's remarks—remarks which were never broadcast. On October 25, McNichol furnished a transcript: 'It will be a matter of attacking, really, J. Edgar Hoover, and asking very rude questions such as why the FBI can find a junkie but cannot find a man who bombs the homes of Negro leaders in the Deep South. They still have not found anyone.'

Concern over Baldwin's criticisms increased as it began to be suspected that he was engaged in writing about the Bureau. In the letter to President Kennedy's assistant (June 6, 1963), Hoover said that 'a confidential source, who has furnished reliable information in the past' had advised that Baldwin was preparing 'a statement' on the FBI, and that he intended to release it to coincide with King's prospectus for 'political action this summer'. Hoover did not reveal, though the Baldwin file does, that the 'source' in this case was a wiretap on the telephone of Stanley Levison, one of King's most senior aides ('a confidential source' is frequently, but not always, code wording for a listening device). The eavesdroppers heard Clarence Jones tell Levison: 'I have seen some statements on the FBI, but I have never seen one like this. He is going to nail them to the wall.' Levison agreed: 'It really will because Baldwin is a name in the news.' The FBI also learned that Baldwin had told Jones, his main link to the

King camp, that the SCLC had a 'blank check to do whatever they wanted' in his newsworthy name. Jones informed Levison proudly that he had 'spent all day Sunday going into some detail' with Baldwin on a programme of political action.

The FBI took a keen interest in Baldwin's putative 'statement'. Just by dwelling on it, they made it grow. Within a few weeks, it had swollen to become an 'article', and by early in the new year had sprouted into a full-length book. Another wiretap, this one on a civil rights foot soldier, revealed that Baldwin intended to use information given to him by Annell Ponder, a woman who, like Jerome Smith, had been badly beaten while taking part in the Freedom Rides in 1961. Ponder had been taken to jail and assaulted by a Negro prisoner at the direction of white policemen. The 'source' (i.e., wiretap) conveyed Ponder's opinion that 'anyone who tells you the FBI is really interested in Mississippi is full of junk'.

Progress on the book continued—even without the participation of the author. It was mentioned in the *New York Herald Tribune* (July 14, 1964), and shortly afterwards an FBI memo stated confidently that 'Dial Press will publish next Spring', a fact discovered 'through established sources at Dial Press'. An informer at the firm, which had been Baldwin's publishers for eight years, said that the book was to be called 'The Blood Counters', and that galley proofs could probably be delivered to the FBI 'in November or December'.

The precise content remained a mystery, but in an interview with the theatre magazine *Playbill*, Baldwin let drop that, like *The Fire Next Time*, 'The Blood Counters' would first be serialized in the *New Yorker*. This begat an FBI summary report on the *New Yorker*. The words 'communist front' were withheld, but 'over the years [it] has been irresponsible and unreliable with respect to references concerning the Director and the FBI'.

When, in 1988, I asked William Shawn, then editor of the *New Yorker*, if he had ever planned to publish an article by Baldwin about the FBI, he replied that he had never heard of it. Likewise, Baldwin's editor of the time at Dial Press, Jim Silberman, had no recollection of such a project. No additional detail about 'The Blood Counters' appears in any book about Baldwin. The main source of information about it is the FBI file.

No action was recommended to be taken against Annell Ponder's torturers, in the memo which recorded her beatings. The moral dimension of the black struggle was not the stuff of which FBI reports were made. Hoover frequently reiterated that the FBI was not a police force. 'Stick to the facts,' he wrote in his book *Masters of Deceit* (1958). 'The FBI is not interested in rumour or idle gossip.' Morality, in the civil rights context, would have seemed to him to tend towards the latter category, as something intangible, subjective. However, he was constantly on the lookout for evidence of 'immorality', in the shape of 'facts' which could be used to undermine significant figures, perhaps even dislodge them. The most notorious example concerns the release of details of Martin Luther King's secret sex life, gathered on tapes from the many listening devices planted around King. The recordings were used in 1964 to try to blackmail King into committing suicide. William Sullivan, the head of Domestic Intelligence, later admitted in his memoir, *The Bureau* (1979), that the FBI was responsible. Sullivan himself arranged for the compilation tape to be sent to the King household on the eve of King's departure for Stockholm to accept the Nobel Peace Prize.

Efforts to smear Baldwin in a similar fashion would prove more difficult, as Baldwin was relatively open about his homosexuality. The qualifier is necessary: in the early 1960s, the fact of homosexuality was unspeakable in public life, and was often left unspoken even among friends. The concept of 'coming out' could not exist, for it had no context (Baldwin played a part in creating it). The subject of homosexuality, linked to the quest for identity, was at the core of his two most recent novels, *Giovanni's Room* and *Another Country*, and to that extent his sexual preferences had been made public. In the mind of Hoover, though, proof of deviance in Baldwin's private behaviour could still be a useful weapon in destroying public confidence, or in setting others in the civil rights movement against him. Within the FBI, there was no questioning the legitimacy of such intrusion. Once a person was on the Security Index, it followed that he was a 'dangerous individual' (or a 'master of deceit'), and that every item of 'derogatory' information was ammunition for the fight.

At the foot of a memo on the phantom book to the Director from one of his assistants, in July 1964, Hoover scrawled a query:

UNITED STATES GO' RNMENT

Memorandum

TO : Mr. DeLoach

DATE: 7-17-64

FROM : M. A. Jones

SUBJECT: JAMES ARTHUR BALDWIN
INFORMATION CONCERNING

ALL INFORMATION CONTAINED
HEREIN IS UNCLASSIFIED
DATE 5-17-89 BY 2382 b 7 J|af

Tolson
Belmont
Mohr
Casper
Callahan
Conrad
DeLoach
Evans
Gale
Rosen
Sullivan
Tavel
Trotter
Tele. Room
Holmes
Gandy

In my memorandum to you dated 6-22-64, I advised the book review section of "The Washington Post" for 6-21-64, announced captioned individual was contemplating at least four future books. Among these will be one about "the F. B. I. in the South." Our New York Office was advised and requested to make discreet checks among its publication sources in an attempt to verify this information. New York was also asked to remain alert to any possibility of securing galley proofs for the Bureau for review purposes.

The 7-14-64, edition of the "New York Herald Tribune" contained additional information concerning this matter. According to it, Baldwin's book will be published next spring; however, it will be featured in "The New Yorker" magazine prior to its publication in book form.

On 7-16-64, the New York Office telephonically advised that an interview with Baldwin appears in the current issue of "Playbill," the official program of the legitimate theater in that city. The article quotes Baldwin as telling the unidentified interviewer he will begin work soon on a long article about the manner in which Negroes are treated by the FBI. He referred to Bureau personnel as "The Blood Counters," which he claimed is the Negroes' nickname for them. New York is forwarding a copy of "Playbill" to the Bureau.

"The New Yorker" over the years has been irresponsible and unreliable with respect to references concerning the Director and the FBI. It has published articles of a satirical nature concerning FBI tours, "The FBI Story" (both the book and the movie) and crime statistics. Baldwin's book, "The Fire Next Time," appeared in the magazine before it was released in book form.

REC- 33 62-108263-29

The matter of Baldwin's contemplated book about the Bureau is being closely followed and you will be kept advised of pertinent developments.

3 JUL 27 1964

RECOMMENDATION:

ENCLOSURE None. For information.

1 - Mr. DeLoach
1 - Mr. Sullivan
HHA:cmk (7)

64 JUL 29 1964

COPY SENT TO MR. TOLSON

CRIME INF.

'Isn't James Baldwin a well-known pervert?' It may have been prompted by the memory of a separate investigation of Baldwin which had taken place in 1962, under statutes relating to 'Interstate Transportation of Obscene Material'. The material at issue was the novel *Another Country*. After some dilly-dallying, no action was taken against the author. Or the question may have arisen as a result of a more recent memo, which recorded a conversation between Baldwin and Hunter Pitts ('Jack') O'Dell. In a deal involving Hoover, and brokered by the Kennedys, O'Dell had been fired from King's SCLC in 1963, because of his left-wing past. The trade-off was, supposedly, that his removal would make it easier for the President and the Attorney General to mediate between civil rights groups and the FBI.

O'Dell was now working for Baldwin, as part of an ever-expanding, fluid staff of assistants, accountants, secretaries, lawyers, all helping the ever-more-prominent writer to weather the storms of fame. O'Dell's duties in the spring of 1964 involved negotiating with Broadway theatre management over Baldwin's play, *Blues for Mr Charlie*, a civil rights drama set in a racially divided town in Mississippi—the first, though not the last, politically motivated work which Baldwin had produced. O'Dell's telephone was tapped, and the confidential source threw up some rich reports. 'It is noted that in greeting O'Dell, Baldwin stated, "Hello, baby, how are you," and in closing the conversation stated that "It's good to hear from you, baby".' A check on the FBI's 'Obscene Log' confirmed the suspicions to which this gave rise. Baldwin mentioned to O'Dell that he had a dinner appointment that evening, with someone (whose name is withheld) whom the Log revealed to be 'another degenerate'.

Of more immediate interest to the Bureau was an earlier conversation between Baldwin and Jones, who only recently had been singing Baldwin's praises to Stanley Levison, right-hand man to King. Through the wiretap on Jones's phone, it was learned (October 10, 1963) that 'Jones told [name withheld] that he had a falling out with James Baldwin, Negro author, last night... Jones said he has been critical of Baldwin's activities and mentioned that Baldwin's sexual propensities have become known.' The SCLC, which staked all its civil rights demands on non-violent action within the law and on a general aura of respectability, could hardly afford to have candid homosexuals close to the seat of power.

In answer to his scribbled question about Baldwin being a pervert, therefore, Hoover received a carefully researched reply:

> It is not a matter of official record that he is a pervert; however, the theme of homosexuality has figured prominently in two of his three published novels. Baldwin has stated that it is also 'implicit' in his first novel, *Go Tell It on the Mountain*.
>
> The *New York Post* published a series of six articles about Baldwin in January 1964... He criticized American heterosexuality, saying it isn't sex at all but 'pure desperation'. He claims American homosexuality is primarily a waste which would cease to exist in effect if Americans were not so 'frightened of it'...
>
> These remarks are similar to others Baldwin has gone on record with regarding homosexuality. While it is not possible to state that he is a pervert, he has expressed a sympathetic viewpoint on several occasions, and a very definite hostility toward the revulsion of the American public regarding it.

This memo could now be set beside another, from late the previous year, when 'a confidential source' advised that Stanley Levison had ridiculed Baldwin's attempts to mount a boycott of department stores over the Christmas-shopping period, in protest at white mob violence in Birmingham. Baldwin's idea was that damaging the commercial sector would lead to pressure for stronger government action in the South. Levison didn't agree. King, the FBI learned, was put off by the 'poetic exaggeration' in Baldwin's approach to race issues. Levison's own view was that Baldwin and Bayard Rustin, a King aide with whom he had become friendly, were 'better qualified to lead a homo-sexual movement than a civil rights movement'. Should a strong alliance between Baldwin and King threaten to emerge in the future, Hoover now knew where to attack it.

Baldwin had a repertoire of responses he would draw on when faced with a crisis too many: he could 'collapse' (a favourite term of self-diagnosis by this stage in his life); he could refer all requests and responsibilities to one of his assistants; or he could flee.

It was flight that he chose at the end of 1964, as his outer obligations multiplied and the inner world, where writing began, seemed to shrink to the dimensions of a miniature ivory tower. In an interview with a West German newspaper in September 1964 (interviews by now far outnumbered written articles), Baldwin threatened to 'emigrate' should Barry Goldwater win the election that year. The interview was clipped and filed by an FBI agent. Goldwater did not win, of course—Lyndon Johnson was returned in a landslide victory to the White House—but Baldwin left anyway.

The FBI went, too. 'On 27/11/65 [name withheld] met James Baldwin at the Hotel Boston, Rome, and shared a room with him.' (They were still sharing, the memo noted, two days later.) Baldwin was booked to speak at the Italian Cultural Institute during the same week, and his comments were monitored. In 1966, he began to spend long periods in Istanbul, having gone there originally five years earlier at the invitation of a Turkish actor, Engin Cezzar, and his wife.

> NY T-2 advised that James Baldwin... arrived at Istanbul, Turkey, by ship on March 29, 1966. During his stay, Baldwin resided with Engin Cezzar, Ayapasa Saray Arkasi 32/3, Istanbul.
>
> NY T-5 advised... during the summer of 1966, Baldwin rented an apartment in the Bebek Section of Istanbul. She found out later that Baldwin was evicted by the landlord for having homosexual parties.

'Turkish Police records' were searched to establish further addresses. By now, Baldwin was the subject of an FBI F#1 Stop Notice, which meant that Bureau sources within the Immigration and Naturalization Service (INS) were obliged 'to immediately notify the FBI if [Baldwin] passes through the area'. Journeys from the United States to Mexico, Canada, France and other destinations were duly logged. Each time a report was filled out, it was likely to be marked 'communist', though no further evidence of Baldwin's membership of any communist organization, or sympathy for communism, had been put forward. Quite simply, the FBI saw no need for it. Even ex-communists who left the Party and spoke out against it—such as the

9/23/63

TO: DIRECTOR, FBI (157-6-34)

FROM: SAC, NEW YORK (157-892)

SUBJECT: RACIAL SITUATION   ALL INFORMATION CONTAINED
           NEW YORK DIVISION   HEREIN IS UNCLASSIFIED
           RACIAL MATTERS   DATE 5/22/89 BY

advised on 9/22/63, that on that date
STANLEY LEVISON conferred with They discussed the stand taken by JAMES BALDWIN and his group
with respect to the Birmingham situation. They agreed that the
entire business of their condemnation of the Presidential
commission to study the Birmingham situation, and also their
idea of boycotting Christmas shopping, were extremely ridiculous.
STANLEY LEVISON expressed the opinion that this group of BALDWIN's
was not "too deep intellectually."

asked what BAYARD RUSTIN's position was with
BALDWIN and LEVISON replied that in his opinion, the two were
better qualified to lead a homo-sexual movement than a civil
rights movement.

3 - BUREAU (157-6-34)(RM)
1 - NY 100-   (414)
1 - NY 100-   (JAMES BALDWIN) (412)
1 - NY 100-A6724   (BAYARD RUSTIN) (424)
1 - NY 100-111180   (STANLEY LEVISON) (414)
1 - NY 157-892   (412)

FTL:mfd (#414)
(9)

SEARCHED ___ INDEXED ___
SERIALIZED ___ FILED ___

SEP 2 3 1963
FBI — NEW YORK

novelist and former friend of Baldwin, Richard Wright, a vehement anti-communist who had contributed to the anthology *The God that Failed* in 1949—were not permitted to disavow their former allegiance, in the eyes of the Bureau.

The nomadic pattern of life, a reaction to the heady political engagement of 1963–4, continued for the rest of the decade. By now, Baldwin's absences from the United States were so frequent and lengthy that FBI interest in him was dwindling, though he remained on the Security Index. The global surveillance involved pestering his personal associates, under false pretences. When he flew from Istanbul to Paris on December 23, 1966, an FBI man attempted to establish his precise whereabouts by calling his literary agent Robert Lantz and pretending to be 'a member of a peace organization soliciting a statement'. (However, 'Mr Lantz would not divulge Baldwin's address'.) When he returned to New York for Christmas the following year, the FBI first learned of his arrival from sources within the INS, and then attempted to confirm that he was staying at his usual address by means of a similar 'pretext telephone call'. They got his sister Paula, who was referred to as 'Mrs Baldwin, subject's wife', only one of many basic errors in reports. At various times, Baldwin was described as a 'former Professor', as the author of the novels 'Go Tell It to the Mountains' and 'Another World', and as living at 'Horation Street' (that is, Horatio Street) at a time when he had already moved out.

The news that he had been contracted by Columbia Pictures to write the screenplay for a film based on the life of Malcolm X triggered a new investigation, with spies from the Los Angeles Field Office making 'discreet enquiries' at the studio to see if a copy of the script could be obtained, and the undercover questioning of postmen and friends (including Truman Capote) to find out about addresses, travel plans and associations with militant groups on the West Coast. Each of these people then became a 'confidential source', and entitled to legal protection under the FBI's view of the Freedom of Information Act. 'When people think of informants, normally they think of paid informants,' says Lesar. 'But the FBI had traditionally regarded anyone who provided it with information as a confidential source. If the FBI calls up James Baldwin's landlord and says, "Hey, is Baldwin in the country?", that guy becomes an FBI informant.'

With Martin Luther King, 1968   ESTHER JACKSON

The Hollywood project ended acrimoniously, and no film about the life of Malcolm X based on Baldwin's script was ever made.

Towards the end of February 1968, he took part in a rally at Carnegie Hall, with Martin Luther King among other speakers, to mark the one-hundredth anniversary of the birth of W. E. B. Du Bois, a guiding spirit of the modern civil rights movement. In a sober suit bought specially for the occasion, Baldwin was photographed with King, looking like a small boy next to his hero. It seems likely that he was never aware of the extent to which he had been deliberately sidelined by the SCLC, which, briefly, in the middle of 1963, had regarded him as a prize. Levison, in particular, was hostile towards him; his view that Baldwin was not 'too deep intellectually' (stated in a telephone conversation recorded by the FBI on October 22, 1963) was not shared by King himself, who nevertheless wished to see him distanced from the organization. According to a taped conversation between Levison and King, the SCLC leader felt that

'Baldwin was uninformed regarding his movement. King noted that Baldwin, although considered a spokesman of the Negro people by the Press, was not a civil rights leader.'

The FBI had several informants in the audience that night, all of whom filed reports. 'Dr Martin Luther King said [sic] tribute to Dr W. E. B. Du Bois and stated that Dr Du Bois would be with him when he and others go to Washington in April.' With him in spirit, the informant meant; or perhaps he or she was unaware that Du Bois had died five years before. In any case, King did not march on Washington for a second time, as planned, to make a renewed appeal to the nation's conscience. He and Baldwin shared a belief that the continuing degradation of blacks demeaned whites as well. 'It is a terrible, an inexorable, law,' Baldwin had preached at the beginning of the decade, 'that one cannot deny the humanity of another without diminishing one's own.' King was shot dead in Memphis just a few weeks after the Carnegie Hall rally, on April 4. Baldwin wrote in *No Name in the Street* that he wore the same new suit to the funeral, adding, with a touch of the very poetic exaggeration which had caused King to separate himself, that it was 'drenched in the blood of all the crimes of my country'.

Three

Appearing on television with David Frost not long after the assassination, Baldwin displayed the odd, riddling manner which was now his accustomed style, in both writing and speech:

> Frost: Are you more conscious now of being black than when you were a child?
> Baldwin: I think you should ask that question of our President.
> Frost: Pardon?

Overcoming his puzzlement, Frost mentioned King's assassin, a drifter and small-time thief. He began to say that 'for every James Earl Ray' (who, after the shooting, had flown to England where he was arrested) there are 'a hundred thousand other' whites who feel differently, but Baldwin interrupted: 'I don't think we want to discuss James Earl Ray, because I don't believe—speaking in my

persona as Sambo—that he could have swum across the Memphis
River all the way to London by himself.'

The conversation ended there, with Baldwin hinting at the
collusion of powerful people in King's murder. At the time, it was
not known publicly that the FBI had sent King the tape containing
recordings of his bedroom exploits (mainly with white women),
accompanied by the suggestive letter: 'King, you're a fraud... You
know what to do...' But in his 'persona as Sambo'—the intuitive
fool—Baldwin would have known of government attempts to destroy
public confidence in prominent black figures, including himself.

These efforts were given renewed impetus in an intensive
campaign which Hoover began in August 1967, eight months before
the assassination, officially known as 'Counterintelligence program
[COINTELPRO], Black Nationalist—Hate Groups'. It was
remounted in the spring of 1968, when the FBI in Washington issued
a memorandum (March 4) urging action to 'prevent the rise of a
messiah who could unify and electrify the militant black nationalist
movement'. King and Stokely Carmichael were singled out for
attention. King was 'a very real contender' for the position of
'messiah', should he 'abandon his supposed obedience to white liberal
doctrines (non-violence) and embrace Black Nationalism'.

King's influence had been severely reduced since the mid-1960s,
but Hoover could think only of stepping up the campaign against him.
According to Sullivan in *The Bureau*, 'Hoover believed that King was
a Communist and he went after him with his biggest guns. No one,
not the Kennedys and certainly not anyone at the Bureau, could stop
the surveillance and harassment to which King was subjected until his
death in 1968.' The 'messiah' memo was distributed to forty-four FBI
field offices (including Memphis), with the instruction that 'imagination
and initiative' should be used in action taken against black groups and
their figureheads. And action was expected. In a novel strategy,
Washington HQ directed local field offices to respond within thirty
days. Thirty-one days after the memo was issued, King was shot.

This little sample of syllogistic presentation does not, of course,
prove that the FBI murdered Martin Luther King. Numerous
investigations by journalists and lawyers (including Lesar, who was
once part of James Earl Ray's legal team), and by a Department of

Justice Task Force, have failed to establish concrete connections. The Task Force, which was set up in 1975 to examine the FBI's harassment of King, and his assassination, found that 'the COINTELPRO campaign was...very probably felonious', but not that Ray had FBI backing.

A House Select Committee Report, published four years later, threw up some startling new details about the Lorraine Motel in Memphis, where King was killed. During a visit to the city to support a strike by garbage workers in the week before the assassination, King had had to make a quick exit from a demonstration that turned violent. He and his entourage took refuge in a nearby Holiday Inn, remaining there until they left town. When the FBI learned of his decision to return to Memphis the following week, to try to repair the bad publicity caused by the riot, Sullivan's Domestic Intelligence division arranged for the release of a 'news item' (initialled by Hoover) to sympathetic press agencies:

> The fine Hotel Lorraine in Memphis is owned and patronized exclusively by Negroes but King didn't go there after his hasty exit. Instead, King decided the plush Holiday Inn Motel, white owned, operated, and almost exclusively white patronized, was the place to 'cool it'.

King had stayed at the Lorraine on visits to Memphis since the 1950s, and it is likely that he would have returned there anyway, without the Bureau's insidious encouragement. The gunman was certainly expecting him. He trained his sights on the balcony on April 4, confident that King would walk across sooner or later, as he did just after 6 p.m.

Speaking to David Frost on television in 1968, Baldwin knew nothing of COINTELPROs, or directions to use 'imagination and initiative' against black 'messiahs', or of FBI coercion to guide King back towards the hotel in which he was murdered; but 'Sambo' did. Sambo relied on—one of Baldwin's favourite lines from scripture— 'the evidence of things not seen'.

After the assassination, Baldwin appears to have been subject to what medical people call 'sympathetic identification' with the victim. Just a few days after King's death, he wrote to Engin Cezzar in Istanbul that he was now 'the black elder statesman', and, more puzzlingly, that he was 'the only mobile black American left'. It is hard to see what he meant, but meaning was all off balance in Baldwin's inner ear. He told the *New York Times* that 'white America appears to be seriously considering the possibilities of mass extermination', and, again and again, raised the spectre of the Reichstag Fire and the Holocaust. He told Cezzar that the FBI had his every change of direction covered, and that his telephone conversations were being taped. In fact, at this time, what little interest the FBI had in Baldwin concerned the ill-starred project to make a film based on the life of Malcolm X.

The following year, he wrote to another friend that he had been ill: 'first the stomach—then the eyes—I never really believed that any of it was physical... I simply panicked, or, in effect, fainted.' After a spell in the American Hospital in Paris, he surfaced in St-Paul, first renting and then buying the old farmhouse on the hillside, which would be his base for the rest of his life. A further perplexing scan of his nervous system shows up in an interview given at the time to the black magazine *Essence*. Baldwin had always had a tendency to mythologize his own past. In the conversation with Ida Lewis, the editor of *Essence*, he makes a number of gnomic comments, punctuated by a flagrant rewriting of the story of his life in Paris on first landing there, broke, in 1948—in the new version, Baldwin lived among 'Algerians and Africans', rather than the young and mostly white Americans and Europeans who sustained him socially and financially. He then uttered the remark which was to become a refrain ever after: 'I loved Medgar. I loved Martin and Malcolm. We all worked together and kept the faith together. Now they are all dead... I'm the last witness—everybody else is dead.'

He believed there was still a role for him, though it was not the traditional writer's role. Passing over the curious claim to be 'the last witness', Lewis pressed him to distinguish between a witness and an observer. 'An observer has no passion,' Baldwin said. 'I don't have to observe the life and death of Martin Luther King. I am a witness to it.'

In October 1963, Baldwin had made a trip to Selma, Alabama, to encourage black citizens to register to vote. The people who turned up were kept in baking heat outside the county courthouse all day long, forbidden to leave the line, surrounded by policemen who carried on a charade of treating Baldwin and his co-organizers as if they were interfering with the rights of would-be voters. 'I will not have these people molested in any way,' the county sheriff kept repeating when Baldwin or one of the others tried to bring refreshments to the queue. After an all-day wait, about twenty, out of 300, were admitted to the courthouse. The others were told to try again.

On his return to New York, Baldwin kept an appointment with Fern Eckman, who was writing a profile of him for the *New York Post*. In a state of nervous agitation, he described what he had witnessed in Selma. 'And all of this is happening, by the way, under the eyes of the FBI. Who are taking *pictures*.'

The pictures were developed and stored in Baldwin's file, turning up twenty-five years later, in Xerox form, on my original FOIA request. He is visible, indistinctly, arguing with the sheriff on the steps of the courthouse, in the company of his brother David and the Student Nonviolent Coordinating Committee leader, James Foreman. The FBI had many of the details of his trip to Selma, including flight number, the name of the person who was to meet him at the airport, the fact that he or she did not turn up, the name of the hotel at which Baldwin was staying, and what telephone calls he had made from there. The incident, together with the earlier one involving the agents who tried to enter his apartment, shows that Baldwin was aware that he was under surveillance almost from the moment it began.

The precise weight of this burden can only be measured by the impression it makes. After 1963, Baldwin began to deteriorate as a writer. Five years later, he would tell Engin Cezzar that he was being shadowed permanently, when, almost certainly, he was not. In this state of mind, every conversation is at risk of being overheard, even when no one is listening. Friends may appear to act in unfriendly ways, appeals from eager college students are confused with pretext telephone calls, and every passer-by taking innocent snaps is working for the FBI.

The writer works out of a private conversation with himself, but the game of shadows makes it likewise difficult to decide which sentence is a true sentence and which a 'poetic exaggeration', which radical creation is a second-hand stereotype, and whether the novel five years in the making, but too often interrupted by the urgencies of politics, is a mirror to the soul or a garrulous shambles. It is hard to write between assassinations, and even harder when everyone— or so it seems—is listening to the writer's private conversation with himself, except the writer.

The FBI formally wound up its investigation of Baldwin on March 25, 1974. No reports had been filed since Hoover's death two years earlier. The campaign was grounded in personal affront, sustained on a misapplication ('communist'), and was probably 'felonious'. In James Lesar's opinion, virtually everything for which the FBI targeted Baldwin was 'protected free-speech activity', covered by the First Amendment to the United States Constitution. 'These files were not compiled for law-enforcement purposes. They are a compendium of every piece of gossip that the FBI picked up through wiretaps and other sources that relate to Baldwin, but none of it relates to illegal activity.'

In the most ruthless reading of the facts, it is possible to conclude that Hoover succeeded in his campaign against Baldwin. He left the country at the height of his influence and at a crucial turning in the struggle for civil rights, when King's power was slipping among a people impatient for change. To several of Baldwin's contemporaries, including Norman Mailer and Jim Silberman, his editor at Dial Press, his decision to leave was misguided. 'I felt that he was wasting his substance being in Europe,' Mailer told me. 'He spent too much time in Europe, when there was so much to write about in America at that time. If he'd gone to Europe and written great books about America, it would have been all right. But he didn't. He went to solve problems in his own life.' (Mailer was not as severe as he might sound. He added: 'One affinity I've always felt with Baldwin is that each of us could be faulted for having spent too much time solving our personal problems.') The FBI was neither happy nor unhappy to see him go, but merely recorded the facts in the neutral tone which characterizes the bulk of FBI paperwork. Sure evidence of his diminishing importance is to be found in the tapering off of his file; only a few memos date from the late 1960s, and a report of June 1971 states that Baldwin is now 'removed from the mainstream of Black Power activities'. There was a brief revival of interest when an interview appeared in *L'Express* in August 1972, in which Baldwin talked about 'making the cities uninhabitable' etc., but that was conducted in Paris, printed in a faraway country in an inaccessible language.

Despite his attempts to align himself with the more militant Black Panthers, and to offer Stokely Carmichael the support of an 'older brother'—so wrote one of the informants at Carnegie Hall that night—Baldwin was left behind when the movement entered its new phase. This was a young, fast-talking, gun-toting leadership; it included Huey Newton, Rap Brown and Eldridge Cleaver, who published a fierce attack on Baldwin in his book, *Soul on Ice*, in 1968: 'There is in James Baldwin's works the most gruelling, agonizing, total hatred of the blacks, particularly of himself, and the most shameful, fanatical, fawning, sycophantic love of the whites that one can find in the writings of any black writer of note in our time.'

When History changed the tune, Baldwin was still dancing the old step. But History changes tunes unpredictably. The FBI of those years continues to be exposed as an organization which regarded itself as being above the law, run by a Director who was obsessed by the communist menace and the sexual peccadilloes of others, and who operated, as his Assistant Director Sullivan later wrote, 'in fear of blacks and social change'.

Baldwin's second act as an American writer was not a happy one; nor, despite the fact that he continued to be productive after 1970, writing two more novels and several works of non-fiction, was it successful. History, though, will refer to something else in him, a quality he himself raised in that conversation with Ida Lewis: 'I always felt that when I was talking publicly...I was talking about people's souls. I was never really talking about political action.' □

THE WOMEN'S
ASHRAM

PHOTOGRAPHS BY DAYANITA SINGH
TEXT BY SUNIL KHILNANI

Nirmala Chakravarty, a young and beautiful Shakta mystic from East Bengal, known to her followers as Anandamayi, first came to the city of Benares in 1928. A ceaseless traveller, she was to make it a home of sorts (as Shiva's city, Benares is of special importance to Shaktas, who are followers of Shiva's female companion, Durga), and gathered a large and devoted following. In the early 1940s, a few years after her husband died, she established in the city an ashram for young girls, a *kanyapeeth*. It was by no means usual for a woman—still less a widow—to penetrate the maze of this most sacred Hindu city. Ashrams were a monopoly of male gurus, with strict rules of initiation and discipleship, and residents were nearly always male. Anandamayi's *kanyapeeth* was—and remains— probably unique in India.

The ashram, a massive abutment of stone walls, white stucco courtyards, rooms, canopies and terraces, with sweeping views across the city and river, was built high above the Ganges just beyond Asi Ghat, where the river begins its long, slow bend northwards. The land was given to Anandamayi by the Maharaja of Benares—he and his sister had become devotees—and the big stone steps that lead down from the ashram to the river were named Anandamayi Ghat. In this most clamorous of cities, busy with the traffic of migrant souls and the display of every aspect of life and death, the ashram became a very private, secluded world.

Anandamayi died in 1982. Over the course of her long life, she counted devotees among the poorest as well as among India's elites. One of her most famous followers was Kamala Nehru—wife of the agnostic Jawaharlal Nehru, and mother of Indira Gandhi. Indira Gandhi herself, from time to time, would turn to Anandamayi for talismans and spiritual relief: indeed, when Mrs Gandhi was sworn in as Prime Minister for the first time in 1966, she made it a point to wear a *rudrakshamala*—a necklace of special wooden beads— given to her by Anandamayi.

The ashram Anandamayi founded has survived her death. Today it houses around forty girls, many of them sent there by their parents in Bengal, and half a dozen senior disciples who instruct and teach them. The girls, who know Anandamayi as Ma, can enter the ashram from the age of six; when they reach eighteen they are free to decide whether to remain there and renounce the world or return to it—as most in fact do. The days begin early, at 4 a.m., with Arati ceremonies—the lighting of oil lamps and singing (the singing carries on throughout the day; that, and the laughter of the girls, is a regular sound), and some formal lessons—in recent years they have started to learn English. The girls attend to everything themselves: cleaning, laundry, cooking (good Bengali vegetarian food without passion-stimulating onions or garlic, all cooked on coal fires). There is no radio, television or newspapers and the girls rarely leave the ashram. One occasion when they do is an annual journey by boat to the Maharaja's palace in Ramnagar. But every day, from their terraces, they can watch the world: burning pyres, marriage ceremonies, children playing, the sunrise across the river. Most visitors to Benares know nothing of the girls' existence. Only from a boat on the river can you sometimes see their hands waving, small and excited, from the terrace.

Outsiders do come to the ashram—but they are confined to the public courtyard and are not given access to the interior where the girls live, learn and play. Until now, the only photographs taken at the ashram have been of its public areas—most notably by that great observer of Benares, Richard Lannoy. Looking at the photographs taken by him, fifty years ago, and those taken by Dayanita Singh in 1998, the constancy of the girls is remarkable: the same cropped hair, bright eyes, a scampish grace. □

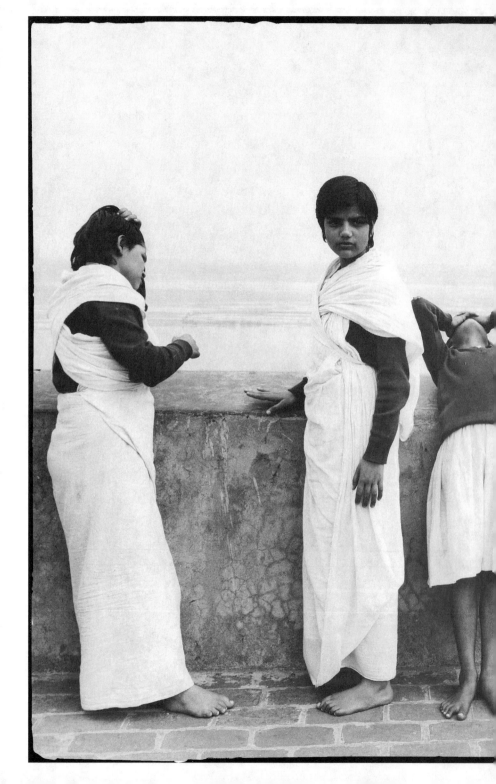

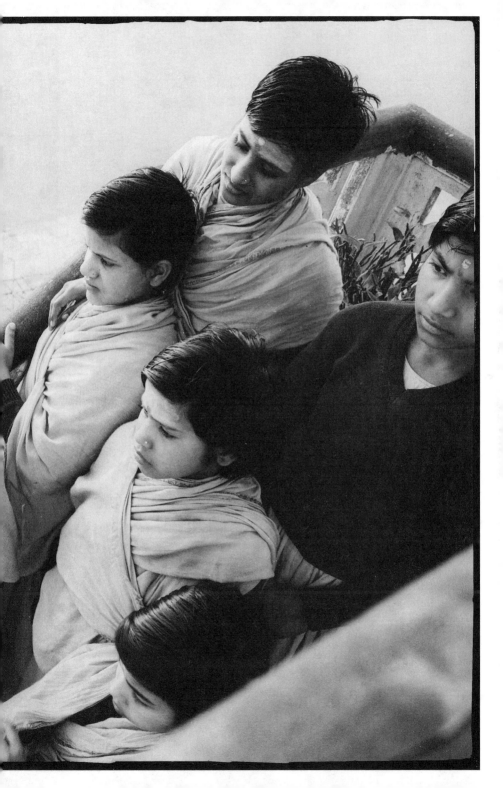

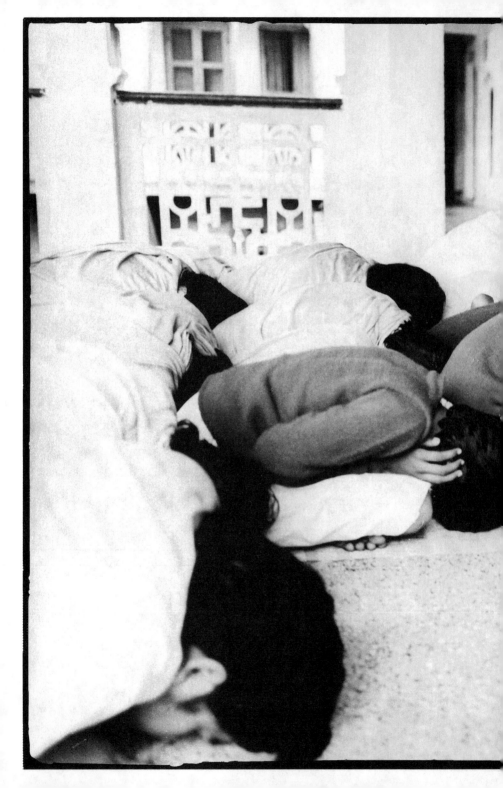

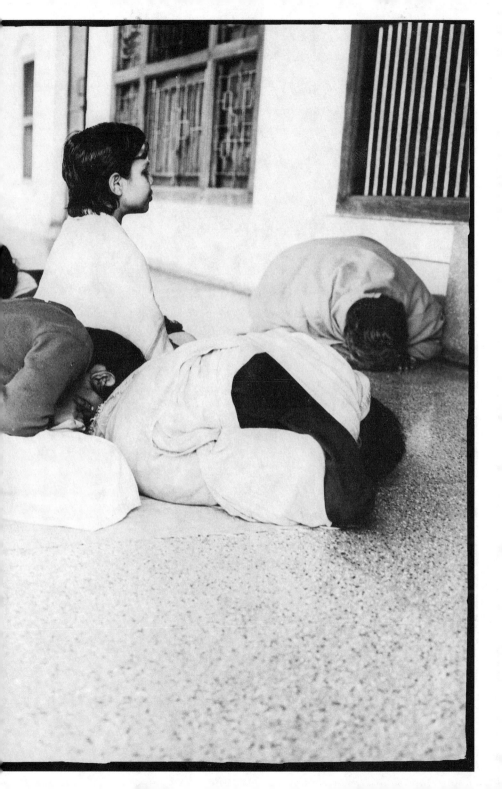

Dinner (डिनर) - रात का भोजन
Lunch (लंच) -
get up (गैट अप) -
Work (वर्क) -
Break fast - नाश्ता
(ब्रेक फास्ट)
Face (फेस) - चेहरा
After (आफ्टर) - बाद
Bed time (बेड टाइम) - सोने के समय
- दिन
- गृह कार्य
- कहना
Son (सन) - बेटा

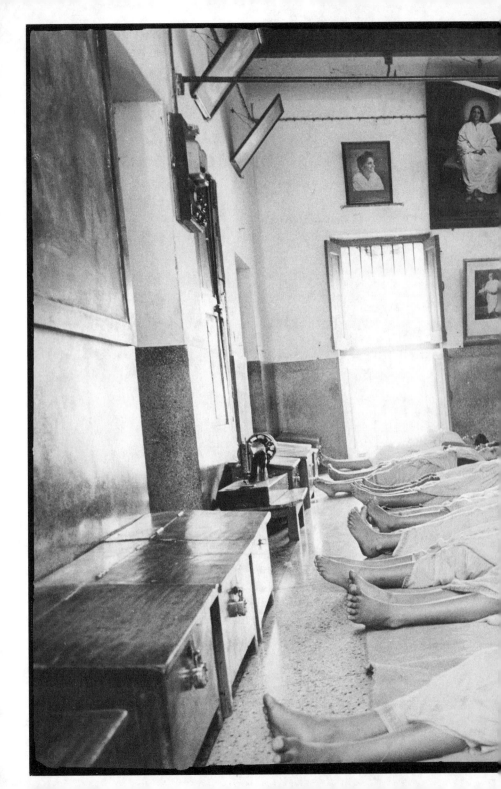

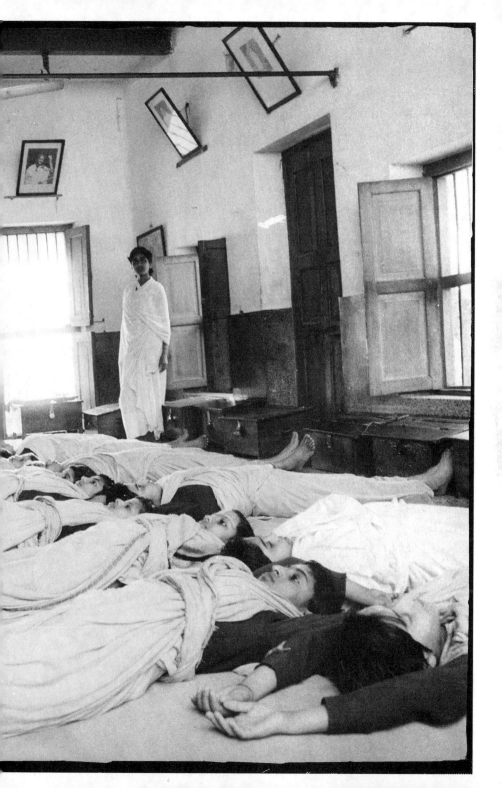

DIEGO GARCIA
Simon Winchester

Turtles rampant: the official coat of arms of the British Indian Ocean Territories

How do you persuade a thousand dogs to walk into a fire? How do you persuade them, as it were, to commit *suttee*? A thousand stray and rather wild dogs at that, all of whom need to be killed for urgent geopolitical reasons, to keep London and Washington happy. On the island of Diego Garcia, on an afternoon of fierce heat in spring 1971, this was the problem facing Sir Bruce Greatbatch, KCVO, CMG, MBE, who was then acting in his capacity as Governor of the Colony of the Seychelles and Commissioner of a newly established and then little-known imperial entity called the British Indian Ocean Territories.

It was hardly the crowning moment of Sir Bruce's long colonial career, which had unrolled its stately way over four decades of administering the subject peoples of King George VI and then his daughter, Queen Elizabeth II, in parts of their empire ranging from northern Nigeria to Barbados. Here, on a tiny and hitherto insignificant speck of coral limestone at a point in the Indian ocean equidistant from Sri Lanka, Mombasa and the Arabian peninsula, Sir Bruce was compelled to supervise, not a Queen's Birthday Party or the opening of a Dominion parliament, but the slaughter of a thousand mongrels.

Sir Bruce had the means at his disposal. On an island which had once harvested its coconut crop to produce coconut oil, there was a long, low brick-built shed known as the coconut calorifier. The shed had two shelves ranged one above the other, the upper to hold the flesh of hundreds of coconuts, the lower to hold the coconuts' husks. By setting the husks on fire, the flesh above would be cooked and its water content (fifty per cent) evaporated until it became copra, an edible fat from which oil can be crushed. An economical system on Diego Garcia—all parts of the nut were used, no extra cost of imported fuel—but one designed for the inanimate. Still, this was to be the pyre. A ton or so of husks were heaped inside and set alight that day, sending up flames and billows of black smoke. Of course, the dogs were recalcitrant: they kept escaping to the beach and turning viciously on their whippers-in.

It took several hours, this great imperial dog-durbar, and must have tested Sir Bruce to the limits of his ingenuity. But eventually, with the aid of rifles, strips of strychnine-laced beef and whips made from palm fronds, the dogs were all herded or dumped dead inside the shed. Whereupon, acting on a plan drawn up as part of the retreat from this particular corner of the British Empire, Sir Bruce had the fires restoked and the calorifier sealed with closely fitting steel plates, and the dogs were promptly—or, according to contemporary reports, really rather slowly—burned or suffocated. An hour or so later, as the sun was going down, their remains were inspected and Sir Bruce was able to declare the Crown Colony of the British Indian Ocean Territories to be utterly empty of all creatures large enough to be a nuisance.

The government of the United States was informed of the fact by diplomatic telegram. Some years before, American generals and admirals had insisted on this emptiness before they would consider building what they then found it convenient to call 'a small communications facility' on the territory's islands. Now a treaty signed between Britain and America in 1966 could be put into effect.

Before the day was out a detachment of Seabees, which had been bobbing about offshore waiting for orders, landed with a dozen mighty earth-moving trucks, their tyres three times as tall as a man. Soon they were churning up the soft pink sand and laying the foundations of what was to become one of the largest and most important foreign military bases America has ever constructed in peacetime. 'Under no circumstances refer to what is being built as a "base",' wrote a nervous official in the British Foreign Office to his ambassadors in Washington and at the United Nations, around the time when the Seabees first ground their way onshore. But a base is very much what was built.

Thirty years later, nearly 4,000 American sailors and contractors live on Diego Garcia. There are two bomber-capable runways, each two and a half miles long; two 'nuclear-cleared berths', and a network of jetties and piers. The lagoon now has deep-water anchorages for thirty ships. The skyline of the island has been speared by arrays of towers, space-tracking domes, oil, petrol and aviation fuel dumps, barracks, weapons ranges, and training areas. By the summer of last year the US government was calling Diego Garcia an 'all but indispensable platform', absolutely central to American strategy for policing a large part of the world and in particular the Middle East.

Diego Garcia got its name from a Portugese navigator in the sixteenth century. On a map it looks like a child's foot—the shapely little heel to the south, the lagoon entrance (which is now one of the world's busiest military seaways) snaking between the big and the first toes. On the water tower by this entrance are painted the words: DIEGO GARCIA: THE FOOTPRINT OF FREEDOM. And yet, despite its appearance as a tropical extension of maritime New Jersey, the island is still most decidedly not American.

It is British, a Crown Colony established in 1965 (and therefore Britain's newest), little different in administrative status from the Falkland Islands, Bermuda, the Caymans or the dozen other relics of empire still ruled from London. Many Stars and Stripes flutter on Diego Garcia, but the flag that flies from the tallest of the island flagstaffs is the Union Jack. The most senior inhabitant of the island is not the resident American Vice-Admiral, but the British officer (normally a naval commander, two ranks below his counterpart) who heads what is known as Royal Naval Party 2002. Or rather, it is either him or, when she visits from London, Margaret Savill, a career diplomat and current BIOT Administrator.

The 4,000 American servicemen who are currently based there are supposed to obey laws (particularly the narcotics ordinances, which are the laws they most frequently break) that are administered on Her Majesty's behalf either by Mr John White, the island Commissioner (who rarely visits, having more onerous tasks relating to the running of British diplomacy in East Africa which he handles from his desk in London); or by Miss Savill (who does go from time to time, taking the regular US Air Force's six-hour C-130 flight from Singapore); or, empowered by ordinance to act for her, by twenty resident Royal Marines, six Scotland Yard policemen and a pair of often bewildered British customs officers who have been flown there on temporary secondment.

How and why did this curiosity come about? Thanks to a legal case, which last year resulted in one of the most damning verdicts on government behaviour ever to be reached by a British court, we now have the full, ignoble story. Six thick volumes of paper, most of them secret government documents, were produced in court. The details disclosed by them show Sir Bruce Greatbatch's behaviour to be relatively benign. Comparing his small dog-holocaust to the other actions by his colonial colleagues, one thing seems clear: getting rid of Diego Garcia's dogs had been perhaps the most difficult *practical* part of the operation. Getting rid of the human beings, some of whom had owned the dogs, had by contrast been a snap.

Someone should have smelled a rat when the British government took the unusual step of creating the new colony in the first place. It happened in the mid 1960s, when London was considering granting independence to its two major island possessions in the western Indian Ocean, the colonies of Mauritius and the Seychelles. The age of Empire was now coming to an end and with it Britain's military bases in the East: bases in Hong Kong, Singapore, on the island of Gan in the Maldives and at Aden on the southern tip of the Arabian peninsula—all of them, sooner or later, were going to have to be abandoned.

Mao's China was then a preoccupation among the West's military strategists; it had recently invaded India and defeated the Indian army in a conflict over national frontiers in the Himalayas. To counter what was perceived as the Chinese threat (and Soviet influence in the Middle East, Africa and India), the USA needed a secure base in the Indian Ocean to replace the British bases; one free of local populations and the unpredictable behaviour of new and possibly unreliable nation states. A secret Anglo-American conference was held in London in February 1964 to discuss these matters. At this conference, officials happily discovered that there was one obscure archipelago in the very middle of the Indian ocean on which the RAF had long ago built a still usable emergency wartime airstrip.

A survey team was promptly dispatched and reported back that the strip, and the island on which it was located, could be turned into an ideal mid-ocean base with the expenditure of a few million pounds. There was plenty of room for a new airfield, there were ample protected waters for anchoring warships, there would be space enough to put barrack-fulls of soldiers and sailors. Moreover, at the time of the conference, the island was still a British colony. Not only that: with the help of some adroit diplomatic footwork, it might still be possible—if everything was kept quiet—to keep it British.

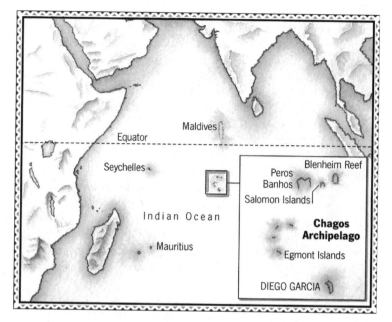

The islands of the archipelago, formally known as the Chagos Islands, were locally known as the Oil Islands—their coconut oil lit the few street lamps of Mauritius and the Seychelles. As a territory it was immense—21,000 square miles of ocean covering the peaks and troughs of an ancient Gondwanaland mountain chain known as Limuria.

Only in eight places had the mountain tops reached close enough to the surface to allow corals to grow and break free of the water. Four of the resulting projections were merely reefs, strewn with the carcasses of wrecked ships and boiling with ragged white lines of surf. The other four were atolls proper, comprising a total of sixty-five individual coral islands arranged in groups: the Salomon Islands and the Peros Banhos atoll to the north, the Egmont Islands at the western edge and, down at the very southern tip of the territory, the curiously foot-shaped atoll, six miles wide and thirteen from heel to toe, of Diego Garcia. It was on this island—where there had once been a coaling station for Australia-bound steamships, and where the transoceanic telephone cable had a repeater station—that the RAF had built its strip.

The Oil Islands had been a minor administrative dependency of Mauritius ever since Britain had taken Mauritius from France as a colony under the First Treaty of Paris in 1814. An independent Mauritius would take the islands as part of its territory. But could an independent Mauritius be trusted to be an ally of the West? There was no certainty of that in 1964. 'It would be unacceptable to both the British and the American defence authorities,' wrote a Colonial Office minister on October 20 of that year, 'if facilities of the kind proposed were in any way to be subject to the political control of ministers of a newly emergent independent state.'

And so a complicated deal was constructed. It was agreed that Mauritius could have all the independence it wanted, and promptly, if, in exchange for a cash payment of £3 million and an informal assurance that the US would look kindly on allowing Mauritian sugar imports, the Oil Islands were excluded—'excised' was the word used—and retained by the British for as long as the British wanted to keep them.

The complexity of the deal that led to the establishment of what were to be called the British Indian Ocean Territories is perhaps understandable; what has only lately come to light is the deviousness— a degree of duplicity that became necessary because of one inconvenient discovery. The Oil Islands, obscure and unknown and forgotten though they might have been, also happened to be populated. People lived there, and had done for generations. That fact brought in its train a whole series of problems.

For a start, the Americans had long insisted that for security reasons there should be no people—either on Diego Garcia itself, or on any other of the outer atolls. The islands should be handed over, 'fully sanitized' and 'swept' (to use the words found in American papers of the time) and ready for the troops and nuclear submarines and bombers that were going to make the colony their home. 'The primary objective in acquiring these islands,' wrote an unnamed British official in an undated memorandum headed 'Objectives', 'is to ensure that Britain has full title to and control over these islands...so that Britain and the United States should be able to clear the Territory of its current population.' The Americans attached great importance to this freedom of manoeuvre and the British authorities went along with this demand.

They assured the Americans that people on the atolls were no more than 'rotating contract personnel'—and just to make sure, in November 1965 and then again six years later, it was arranged for laws to be passed (actually, this being a colony, ordinances were written, without the requirement for any parliamentary consultation) which made it illegal for anyone to come to the islands ever again—or, indeed, to be there in the first place—without a permit. Anyone who was there could be deported, and put in prison while awaiting deportation—or, in the magisterial tones of the Order, 'while awaiting removal...be kept in custody, and while so kept shall be deemed to be in lawful custody'.

The American requirement was one thing. The United Nations was quite another. Then as now the UN took a severe view of the sovereignty of any populated part of the world being arbitrarily changed without the inhabitants being consulted. The establishment of a new colony, with a brand new colonial citizenry, would need to have the status of its people (whether they were agitating for self-government, for example) regularly reported to a UN committee—a requirement agreed to by most of the world since the great decolonizations of the 1950s and 60s.

As early as May 1964 the British were aware of how anti-imperialist forces could seize and spread the news of a new colony. 'Our partition of colonial territories against the will of the populace for UK-US strategic purposes would give the Soviet bloc a golden opportunity to attack us with Afro-Asian support,' wrote an official in the Foreign Office Permanent Under-Secretary's department to his British opposite number at the UN in New York. 'Major damage would also be done to our general reputation vis-à-vis the Afro-Asian world; and we should have given the Communists an opportunity to damage our reputation very seriously indeed.'

But none of these problems would have unduly vexed the British if the islands had indeed been peopled only by rotating contract workers. If that had been the case, then so far as the Americans were concerned, the workers could have been told that their contracts were up, asked to leave, and their return for further work prohibited—brutish behaviour perhaps, but not illegal. And if the inhabitants had been merely passing through—if they had been Mauritians and Seychellois sent over by the company that worked the islands, the

Chagos Agalega Oil Company, to work in the company copra mills and on the calorifiers and on pressing the oil—then the UN could either have been told of this fact in a perfunctory way, or not have been told at all. If the islanders had been transients, the UN's requirements regarding transfer of sovereignty and regular reporting would not have applied.

Were they in fact transients? A Colonial Office official reported in 1964 that a 'small number of people were born there and, in some cases, their parents were born there too'. This set off a flurry of alarm. More research was carried out—and the further discovery was made that the people who lived on the Chagos Islands were not in the main Mauritian and Seychellois but of East African origin, descendants of slaves who had been brought over in the early nineteenth century from Madagascar, Somalia and Mozambique.

There were more than 1,500 of these Chagos islanders. They spoke Creole. They were physically small and wiry. Most disturbing to the officials was the realization that a very large number of them were technically British subjects. Any who had been born on the islands and whose parents had been born there too were indisputably subjects of the Crown. What was more, many of them apparently knew of their status—a visitor in 1955 noted that the islanders were 'lavish with their Union Jacks' and they had serenaded him with a ragged version of the British national anthem, sung in English 'with a heavy French accent'.

The discovery of the presence of 1,000 or more black, wiry, Creole-speaking Britons on islands that the British Government had promised to deliver to the Americans 'swept clean' startled the officials in London. There was panic and—from the very beginning—there was intentional duplicity.

'The intention is that none of them should be regarded as being permanent inhabitants,' was one of the earliest policy suggestions, written within days of the discovery in November 1965 by a member of the Colonial Office (which was merged with the Foreign Office in 1968). So far as the UN was concerned, another Colonial Office official wrote, 'I would advise a policy of "quiet disregard"—in other words, let's forget about this one until the United Nations challenge us on it.'

Diplomats suggested that the islanders be issued with documents showing their status as belonging to Mauritius or the Seychelles—even though they didn't—in the hope of convincing both the UN and the islanders that the British had no need to 'safeguard their democratic rights'. This might, the diplomat conceded, 'be rather transparent'. Another colleague concurred, though he noted that there was in the Colonial Office 'a certain old-fashioned reluctance to tell a whopping fib, or even a little fib, depending on the number of permanent inhabitants'.

Nonetheless, a fibbing policy began to take shape. London's senior civil servants grew more candid. The Permanent Under-Secretary at the Colonial Office was Denis Greenhill—later elevated to the House of Lords as Baron Greenhill of Harrow. In August 1966 he had his secretary, Patrick Wright—later Sir Patrick—send to the British Mission at the UN a note from the Colonial Office which incorporated a gentlemen's club kind of joke.

> We must surely be very tough about this. The object of the exercise was to get some rocks which will remain ours; there will be no indigenous population except seagulls, who have not yet got a Committee (the Status of Women Committee does not cover the rights of Birds).

Having presumably chuckled at this little moment of drollery, Greenhill then added, in his own hand, this remark:

> Unfortunately, along with the Birds go some few Tarzans and Men Fridays, whose origins are obscure, and who are being hopefully wished on to Mauritius etc. When this has been done I agree we must be very tough...

The policy towards BIOT's population from now on would be that implied by the two strands of thinking in these private documents. There would be no indigenous population; the existing population would be 'wished' on to Mauritius.

Five years later, that is exactly what happened. Over a period of eighteen months beginning in 1971, a flotilla of boats entered the various harbours of the scattered atolls of the Chagos Islands and evacuated the islanders. Diego Garcia—and its dogs—was the first to be 'swept'. The outer inhabited islands—Peros Banhos, Salomon—followed later. The entire population was dumped on the dockside of Port Louis in Mauritius, the island where they still live.

Despite a British ruling that 'no journalists shall be allowed on the Chagos Archipelago', I went there once, illegally, and spent a fortnight snooping around. My visit was in 1985, and it is referred to in the Foreign Office papers—'he arrived in a yacht…was refused by immigration authorities…and sent on his way.' Like so much else in the Foreign Office submissions, the remarks are not quite accurate.

I did indeed arrive on a yacht, a thirty-foot Australian-registered steel schooner from Cochin, in South India. I first spent ten days on Boddam Island: of all the islands in the Salomon atoll, the one that most obviously had once been populated. It was a summertime idyll—empty beaches and a warm sea—except that I seemed never to be quite alone: a C-130 from the Diego Garcia base flew low overhead each afternoon, its crew taking photographs of what I was doing, which was idly exploring a tiny island, making notes, drawing maps and sketching the buildings.

There was a street of small two-room cottages, a church and a cemetery containing the tomb of a woman named Mrs Thompson who had died in 1932. There was a copra-crushing mill, with rusty cog-wheels and pockmarked boilers and hardwood pestle-and-mortars where the coconut oil had been pressed. Also a small railway for taking the drums down to the pier, which now sagged wearily among a grove of sea-grape trees. Old lighters were still drawn up on the beach, as well as harnesses for the mules which had helped drag the trucks down to the loading stage.

The most prominent building was a rather splendid little mansion, built in what looked like the French colonial style. It had three floors, verandas, pergolas, a garden shed, a lawn. On one wall I found a picture of a pretty debutante from Wiltshire, cut from a 1971 issue of *Country Life*. There were four yellowed volumes of *The Times History of the War*, and a copy of Pushkin in German.

In the cottages there were dishes and saucepans, toys, rotting bundles of clothes and shoes and outside, in a clucking huddle of excitement at my unexpected arrival, scores of chickens, all with the unkempt look of domestic fowl gone native.

No, these were manifestly not the homes of 'rotating contract personnel', whatever the faraway colonial rulers in London might have wanted the Americans and the 'Afro-Asian community' at the UN to think. This was an old and long-settled village, and quite a prosperous village too—a community where there had been church services, weddings and burials and christenings, where people had read books, played games, worked and saved and made plans for the future. One of the last, according to a history of the islands (*Limuria* by Robert Scott), had been a scheme by a woman resident to turn Boddam Island into a free port where trans-Indian liners could call and their passengers be tempted by duty-free crystal and whisky, after swimming with the manta rays in the baby-blue lagoon. It was easy to see the temptations of the place.

After ten days of languor, I decided to head down to Diego Garcia itself. I spent a day and night sailing over the choppy shallows of the Chagos Bank and managed to sneak into the lagoon and moor myself among the warships and the atomic submarines. When the British immigration officers discovered me, they were furious: they had in their briefcases faxed copies of letters the Foreign Office had written to me two years before, formally refusing me permission to come, and now they waved them at me and insisted that I leave.

But my skipper, a tough young Australian woman, drily informed the immigration men that she was claiming the lagoon as a 'port of refuge', as was her mariner's right, and that she would be staying on Diego Garcia for at least the next two days. And so we dropped anchor; there was nothing the authorities could do as international maritime law prevails even in Diego Garcia.

The Americans were friendly enough. After the British officials' boat had burbled away to the shore, some of the crew of two American ships—the command ship *La Salle* and the atomic submarine *Corpus Christi*—came across in their liberty boats, took us aboard and showed us around. Inside the atoll lay an armada that made Pearl Harbor look puny. Dozens of supply ships rode at anchor, their decks loaded with tanks, rockets, trucks, earth movers and fuel bowsers, each ship judiciously separated from its neighbour by a space known as the 'explosion arc' in case of accidental detonation. There were frigates, destroyers and marine carriers. All kinds of aircaft landed and took off from the runway: fighters, bombers, fuel tankers and tank killers. It was a relief to put to sea again, into the thousands of miles of empty ocean which come between Diego Garcia and any of its potential targets on land.

I have never been allowed back: when I applied to go there legally in 1993, permission was refused by the Foreign Office in London.

The closest I have been to the islands since is Mauritius. There, late last year, I met a woman, Rosalyn Rabrin, who for almost thirty years, since she was ten years old, has lived in a windowless tin shack in a shabby area of Port Louis called Cassis. The shack measures twelve feet by fifteen, and, when the Mauritian sun beats down, is insufferably hot. She lives with her husband Rosemont, a casual labourer on the docks, and their four children—two of whom, fifteen-year-old Sharma and eleven-year-old Martina, were with her on the day we met. The living space was entirely taken up with two beds, a chair and a wardrobe (there was no room for a table): there was a single light bulb; and when the family eats, or when the children do their schoolwork, they do so outside, on the packed dirt of the yard.

Mrs Rabrin is, by law, by birth and by choice, a British subject. She and her children have passports that declare them to be, just like Gibraltarians or St Helenians or Anguillans, British Dependent Territories Citizens, a curiously British underclass of citizen (by contrast all citizens of French possessions are fully French) who will possibly be—one day—legally able to live full-time in Britain: the House of Commons is still considering this idea. For now, though, she lives in the same shack that accommodated her when she arrived in Mauritius by ship from Boddam Island.

She grew up in the narrow street of two-room cottages I had seen, and she remembered it well. There had been a shop, which was open once a week. She showed me a snapshot of the church, and another of the manager's house. She remembered watching the men harnessing the mules to pull the oil barrels down to the quay. She and her girlfriends, who went to primary school on the island, used to swim beside the lighters as they pulled out to the oil ship anchored in mid-lagoon. The vessel was invariably the *Zambezia*, which could reach Mauritius in four days, and sometimes, she said, took passengers. More often the boat that took men back and forth to Port Louis was the *Nordvaer*, or a smaller craft called the *Isle of Farquhar*, which did a three-monthly supply run to all of the islands.

She also remembered the day the villagers were rounded up and told they had to leave.

It was in the summer of 1971. The previous September a Foreign Office official had written an order for the islanders to be deported from their own homes, and had written an Ordinance—no parliamentary approval needed—that sought, among other things, 'to maintain the fiction that the inhabitants…are not a permanent or semi-permanent population'. The government had decided first to cut off the islanders' employment: for £1 million they bought out the islanders' sole employer, the Chagos Agalega Oil Company, and formally closed it down. She remembered the officials who arrived on the deportation boat that summer morning bringing pieces of paper which they gave to the adults: no doubt these were copies of the Ordinance under which the removal was to be accomplished.

'We were told they were going to close down the islands,' she told me, her rapid Creole translated by my taxi driver. 'I am not sure what I thought. My mother and father were quite angry, I remember. We got our stuff from the house, and we were put on the boat by about evening-time. We were sealed down below, in a big iron hold. They put the horses and the mules on the deck above—I remember the terrible noise they made, clattering about up above.

'We had dogs, but we had to leave them behind. I was very upset. I didn't know why we were being taken away. No one had done anything wrong. Everyone was still working—they had been crushing oil on the very day we were ordered on to the ship.

'We left after dark, so I can't remember seeing anything. I don't think there was a porthole, in any case. It took three days to get to Mauritius. There was nothing to eat, and very little to drink. I remember people squeezing flannels and cloths to get rain water to drink. It was terrible. And then we arrived at Port Louis, and someone gave my father some money, and we were told to find a home. And that was that. We never felt the people here wanted us. My father never had a proper job. We've never fitted in.'

I asked her if she wanted to go home. I suggested that she now lived in a city full of possibilities—for her daughters, at least, if not for her. Back on Boddam Island there was nothing. Just ruins. Did she really want to go back?

'Yes,' she said. 'Without any doubt at all. Maybe not to stay forever. But we all want to go back. It is home, even if it is a simple place. I want to see it again, and remember. And our children want to go too.' The two girls nodded their heads in vigorous agreement. 'No doubt at all,' said their mother. 'We want to go.'

At the time I asked the question it had suddenly become—at long last—a highly pertinent enquiry. Because in 2000, after three decades of legal wrangling, it was finally beginning to look as though the islanders might be able to return, to reclaim what they lost when the British government decided forty years ago that 'no indigenous population shall remain' on the islands of the archipelago.

The plight of the people whom the Mauritians call *'les Ilois'* has received only scant and intermittent attention over the years. The *Washington Post* first broke the story in 1975, when a reporter visiting the island heard about 2,000 British subjects who were mysteriously penned up in a slum near the docks. (News of the various British proclamations and ordinances pertaining to the islanders was always shielded from the British public by being published only in the *BIOT Gazette*, an official government publication of necessarily very limited circulation.)

I followed the story up—I was based in Washington at the time for the *Guardian*—and found out that Britain had managed to conceal the $14 million it was paid for the fifty-year lease on the islands by persuading the Americans to disguise the cost as a discount on the research and development charges for a new generation of Polaris nuclear missiles then being sold to the Royal Navy. There were desultory congressional hearings in response to this revelation. Senator

Edward Kennedy referred to 'a clear lack of human sensitivity'; the *New York Times* made much of how 'depressing' the story was 'for anyone who wants to believe in the essential decency and honesty of the British government'; and a film was made and shown on British television which used original Central Office of Information black-and-white footage from the 1950s showing the undeniably settled condition of the locals, and their state of impoverished happiness.

But little else was done. The British paid out £4 million as compensation to the islanders in the mid 1980s when it was politically appropriate to be seen to be doing something. But there was never any mention of the possibility of their being allowed to go home. The US Airforce flew a group of defence correspondents—who must be among the most malleable and cravenly respectful of all journalists—to Diego Garcia for just five hours to report on its technological wonders. 'The Malta of the Indian ocean,' wrote one. 'A place of incalculable strategic significance,' said another.

And that, essentially, was how the status quo was quietly maintained for thirty years. However unfortunate the islanders may have been, however shabbily they may have been treated, their grievance and exile were insignificant when set against the military needs and security of the West, and particularly the US. Or to put it another way: the end, in this case, amply justified the means.

This smug quietude—much cherished by the British Foreign Office and the Pentagon—was shattered last year when Olivier Bancoult, a mild-mannered, middle-aged islander who now works for the Mauritian Electricity Board, won leave—and British legal aid—to fight a case against the British government. He made the claim, in particular, that Section 4 of the BIOT Immigration Ordinance of 1971—the order under which the islanders were removed—was illegal. The Ordinance states baldly: 'No person shall enter the Territory or, being in the Territory, shall be present or remain in the Territory, unless he is in possession of a permit or his name is endorsed on a permit...' The fact that 'no person' meant in this case 'the inhabitants' of the islands struck Olivier Bancoult as manifestly unjust: it meant that the law, as in medieval times, had allowed people to be expelled from their own country. Surely, he sought to say (and had the British taxpayers' money with which to say it), it ought not to be.

The case was fought by the noted South African barrister and civil rights champion Sir Sydney Kentridge. Bancoult's solicitor, Richard Gifford, was from the firm of Bernard Sheridan, a lawyer who has himself long been interested in the plight of the islanders. Few at first thought the court would permit the case to proceed. David Pannick, the QC engaged by the Foreign Office, made many persuasive arguments about the need for the case to be heard by the Supreme Court of BIOT—comprising a semi-retired judge who lives and holds court in Gloucestershire—and not the High Court.

But in the end the High Court did agree to hear Sir Sydney plead Bancoult's case—and on November 3, 2000, Lord Justice Laws and Mr Justice Gibbs reached an astonishing verdict. Citing the Magna Carta and its ancient provisions about the illegality of deporting any man from his own home, the court unanimously decided that Section 4 of the BIOT Immigration Ordinance was unlawful, that it should be quashed, and that Mr Bancoult and the islanders who were now living, like Rosalyn Rabrin and her neighbours, in the slums of Mauritius and the Seychelles, should in consequence be allowed to go home.

The British Foreign Secretary, Robin Cook, announced that the government would not appeal against the ruling. Later the same day, the Foreign Office published a new Immigration Ordinance which confined the banning order only to the island of Diego Garcia itself. For the rest of the Chagos Archipelago, anyone who held a British Dependent Territory Citizenship passport because of his or her connection with the islands could now go and come as he or she pleased. Mr and Mrs Rabrin and her children, in other words, may now go back home to Boddam Island. They can go to their little cottage, reopen the shop, clear the garden at the church and weed old Mrs Thompson's grave, and stay where Rosalyn herself was born, for as long as they like.

As I write, the whole subject of the British Indian Ocean Territory is awash in a sea of complications and recriminations. The British are shamed and embarrassed. The Mauritians are bewildered. And the Americans, not entirely unreasonably, are furious. The

Pentagon, after all, had accepted in good faith that the British had entirely 'sanitized' the archipelago and that it would remain so until the US lease on Diego Garcia had expired.

Eric Newsom, the US Assistant Secretary of State for Political-Military Affairs, wrote to his equivalent in the British Government last June that settlements on the outer islands 'would...immediately raise the alarming prospect of the introduction of surveillance, monitoring and electronic jamming devices that have the potential to disrupt, compromise or place at risk vital military operations' conducted from Diego Garcia. Terrorists could operate from within the territory.

> For the first time in the history of our military co-operation on Diego Garcia, significant personnel and other assets would be required solely for the purposes of protecting the forces, materials and facilities located there. Initiation of such requirements on the island would, beyond the considerable expense for both of our governments, possibly entail reconfiguration of the base facilities...

No American officials have spoken since about the problem thrown up by the court verdict. It was mentioned in only the most perfunctory manner by the newspapers—last November they were much more concerned with the US presidential election. I was in Mauritius at this time and there met an American naval officer who spoke disdainfully of 'that Mickey Mouse court' in London, and the 'total irrelevance' of the judges' decision.

We were having the conversation on the Port Louis dockside, watching a large American logistics ship, the USS *Bob Hope*, dock with 500 sailors on leave from the base. No, he said, noone would be going back, not to any of the islands, so long as there was any American military presence on Diego Garcia. Given the state of the world, he added, that was likely to be for a very long time.

According to Olivier Bancoult and his lawyers—and to what British diplomats are now saying privately too—Americans holding such views are going to be sorely disappointed. For islanders will be going back to their islands, and very soon. The consequences could be extraordinary. The population of Chagos Islanders in Mauritius and the Seychelles is believed to have grown to about 5,000 adults and children. If many of them return, a whole new colony will need to be created. In a strange revival of Victorian imperialism, Britons will have to go out to Boddam Island and to Peros Banhos Atoll and build things: an administration building, a small network of roads and sewers, a police station, a court, a school, a small cottage hospital, a radio station—all so that the returning islanders can have the basic services expected by British citizens. There will have to be employment, too—maybe copra or coconut oil; or—most keenly supposed—tourism.

As I write, the Foreign Office is said to be 'studying all possibilities'.   □

Royal Festival Hall
Queen Elizabeth Hall
Purcell Room

LIVE Literature+Talks
Spring 2001 Highlights

Thursday 5 April, 7.30pm, Queen Elizabeth Hall
MARTIN AMIS WITH MARK LAWSON

Martin Amis will read from his new book, *War Against Cliché* and discuss his career as novelist and critic with Mark Lawson, *Guardian* columnist and BBC broadcaster.

Wednesday 11 April, 7.30pm, Purcell Room
ADAM PHILLIPS WITH JOHN CAREY

In *Houdini's Box*, Adam Phillips explores our fascination with ideas of escape, from Harry Houdini to Emily Dickinson. Phillips will discuss this book and his other works with critic and broadcaster John Carey.

Tuesday 17 April, 7.30pm, Purcell Room
AMY TAN

A rare UK appearance by the internationally acclaimed bestselling novelist, Amy Tan. She will read from her new novel, *The Bonesetter's Daughter*, a story of the relationship between a mother and daughter, set in San Francisco and pre-war China.

Monday 7 May, 7.30pm, Purcell Room
PAUL MULDOON WITH LAVINIA GREENLAW

One of the most influential poets of his generation, Paul Muldoon will be coming to the South Bank to read from his newly published, *Poems 1968-1998*. He will discuss his development as a poet with writer Lavinia Greenlaw.

Tuesday 15 May, 7.30pm, Purcell Room
FIFTY YEARS OF THE ROYAL FESTIVAL HALL: LOOKING TO THE FUTURE OF CIVIC SPACE In association with the RIBA Architecture Gallery

Celebrating the 50th birthday of Britain's largest centre for the arts, our distinguished panel will discuss the prospects for public building in the new century. The event will be chaired by *Observer* architecture critic Deyan Sudjic.

Saturday 30 June, 7.30pm, Purcell Room
ELAINE SHOWALTER

Elaine Showalter's new book, *Inventing Herself: Claiming a Feminist Intellectual Heritage*, argues that feminists need to reclaim their icons in order to gain a sense of the past. Who are our feminist icons? Join the discussion with our special guests.

**All Purcell Room tickets £7.50 (concessions £5), QEH £8 (concessions £5.50)
Granta reader offer: All tickets £5 (concessions £3) when you buy tickets for two or more events from the Spring 2001 Highlights series. Please mention this offer when booking.**

Box Office 020 7960 4242
Book Online www.rfh.org.uk

Royal Festival Hall, London SE

Join our ebulletin list, email: Literature &Talks@rfh.org.uk

50 Royal Festival Hall

THE ARTS COUNCIL

sbc

Restless
Americans

Even the Rhinos Were Nymphos
Best Nonfiction
Bruce Jay Friedman

"This is one of the things that must be appreciated about Mr. Friedman: he got to a lot of stuff first. . . . Black humor? He practically invented the genre. . . . Every so often an undervalued writer is rediscovered. . . . Why should [Friedman] suddenly seem hip again? Maybe because he always has been. . . . His writing is so funny—and deceptively effortless—critics often liken it to a stand-up comedy routine."—Rick Marin, *New York Times*
Cloth $25.00

Restless Nation
Starting Over in America
James M. Jasper

"Jasper's thesis—that the desire, even the compulsion, to be on the move is what defines an American character—is strong and tantalizing. . . . Jasper does not restrict himself to a single discipline or line of argument, but dazzles readers with a stunning combination of literary critique, cultural analysis and economic estimation."—*Publishers Weekly*
Cloth $25.00

Available in bookstores.
The University of Chicago Press
www.press.uchicago.edu

THE LAZY RIVER
Ryszard Kapuscinski

TRANSLATED FROM THE POLISH
BY KLARA GLOWCZEWSKA

Ryszard Kapuscinski

Iam met in Yaoundé by a young Dominican missionary named Stanislaw Gurgul. He will take me into the forests of Cameroon. 'But first,' he says, 'we will go to Bertoua.' Bertoua? I have no idea where this is. Until now I had no idea it even existed! Our world consists of thousands—no, millions—of places with their own distinct names (names, moreover, that are written or pronounced differently in different languages, creating the impression of even greater multiplicity), and their numbers are so overwhelming that travelling around the globe we cannot commit to memory even a small percentage of them. Or—which also often happens—our minds are awash with the names of towns, regions, and countries that we are no longer able to connect meaningfully with any image, view or landscape, with any event or human face. Everything becomes confused, twisted, blurred. We place the Sodori oases in Libya instead of in Sudan, the town of Tefé in Laos instead of in Brazil, the small fishing port of Galle in Portugal instead of where it actually lies—in Sri Lanka. The oneness of the world, so unachievable in the realm of empirical reality, lives in our minds, in the superimposed layers of tangled and confused memories.

It is 350 kilometres from Yaoundé to Bertoua, along a road that runs east, towards the Central African Republic and Chad, over gentle, green hills, through plantations of coffee, cacao, bananas and pineapples. Along the way, as is usual in Africa, we encounter police guard posts. Stanislaw stops the car, leans his head out of the window, and says: *'Eveche Bertoua!'* (the bishopric of Bertoua!) This has an instantaneous and magical effect. Anything to do with religion—with the supernatural, with the world of ceremony and spirits, with that which one cannot see or touch but which exists, and exists more profoundly than anything in the material world—is treated with great seriousness here, and immediately elicits reverence, respect and a little bit of fear. Everyone knows how toying with something higher and mysterious, powerful and incomprehensible, ends: it ends badly, always. But there is more to it. It is about the way in which the origins and nature of existence are perceived. Africans, at least those I've encountered over the years, are deeply religious. *'Croyez-vous en Dieu, monsieur?'* I would always wait for this question, because I knew that it would be posed, having been asked it so many times already. And I knew that the one questioning me would at the same time be observing me carefully, registering every twitch of my face. I realized the seriousness of this moment, the meaning with which it was imbued. And I sensed that the way in which I answered would determine our relationship. And so when I said, 'Oui, j'en crois' (yes, I believe), I would see in his face the relief this brought him, see the tension and fear attending this scene dissipate, see how close it brought us, how it allowed us to overcome the barriers of skin colour, status, age. Africans valued and liked to make contact on this higher, spiritual plane, to which often they could not give verbal definition, but whose existence and importance each one sensed instinctively and spontaneously.

Generally, it isn't a matter of belief in any one particular god, the kind one can name, and whose appearance or characteristics one can describe. It is more an abiding faith in the existence of a Highest Being, one that creates and rules and also imbues man with a spiritual essence that elevates him above the world of irrational beasts and inanimate objects. This humble and ardent belief in the Highest Being trickles down to its messengers and earthly representatives, who as a consequence are held in special esteem and granted reverential acceptance. This privilege extends to Africa's entire multitudinous layer of clergymen from the most varied sects, faiths, churches and groups, of which the Catholic missionaries constitute only a small percentage. For there are countless Islamic mullahs and marabouts here, ministers of hundreds of Christian sects and splinter groups, not to mention the priests of African gods and cults. Despite a certain degree of competition, the level of tolerance between them is astonishingly high, and respect for them among the general population universal.

That is why, when Father Stanislaw stops the car and tells the policemen, 'Eveche Bertoua!' they don't check our documents, do not inspect the car, do not demand a bribe. They only smile and make a consenting gesture with their hand: we can drive on.

After a night in the chancery building in Bertoua, we drove to a village called Ngura, 120 kilometres away. Measuring distances in kilometres, however, is misleading and essentially meaningless here.

If you happen upon a stretch of good asphalt, you can traverse that distance in an hour, but if you are in the middle of a roadless, unfrequented expanse, you will need a day's driving, and in the rainy season even two or three. That is why in Africa you usually do not say, 'How many kilometres is it?' but rather 'How much time will it take?' At the same time, you instinctively look at the sky: if the sun is shining, you will need only three, four hours, but if clouds are advancing and a downpour looks imminent, you really cannot predict when you will reach your destination.

Ngura is the parish of the missionary Stanislaw Stanislawek, whose car we are now following. Without him, we would never be able to find our way here. In Africa, if you leave the few main roads, you are lost. There are no guideposts, signs, markings. There are no detailed maps. Furthermore, the same roads run differently depending on the time of year, the weather, the level of water, the reach of the constant fires.

Your only hope is someone local, someone who knows the area intimately and can decipher the landscape, which for you is merely a baffling collection of signs and symbols, as unintelligible and bewildering as Chinese characters to a non-Chinese. 'What does this tree tell you?' 'Nothing!' 'Nothing? Why, it says that you must now turn left, or otherwise you will be lost. And this rock?' 'This rock? Also nothing!' 'Nothing? Don't you see that it is telling you to make a sharp right, at once, because straight ahead lies wilderness, a wasteland, death?'

In this way the native, that unprepossessing, barefoot expert on the writing of the landscape, the fluent reader of its inscrutable hieroglyphics, becomes your guide and your saviour. Each one carries in his head a small geography, a private picture of the world that surrounds him, a most priceless knowledge and art, because in the worst tempest, in the deepest darkness, it enables him to find his way home and thus be saved, survive.

Father Stanislawek has lived here for years, and so guides us without effort through this remote region's intricate labyrinth. We arrive at his rectory. It is a poor, shabby barracks, once a country school but now closed for lack of a teacher. One classroom is now the priest's apartment: a bed and a table, a little stove, an oil lamp.

The other classroom is the chapel. Next door stand the ruins of a little church, which collapsed. The missionary's task, his main occupation, is the construction of a new church. An unimaginable struggle, years of labour. There is no money, no workers, no materials, no effective means of transport. Everything depends on the priest's old car. What if it breaks down, falls apart, stops? Then everything will come to a standstill: the construction of the church, the teaching of the gospel, the saving of souls.

Later, we drove along the hill tops (below us stretched a plain covered in a thick green carpet of forest, enormous, endless, like the sea) to a settlement of gold diggers, who were searching for treasure in the bed of the winding and lazy Ngabadi river. It was afternoon already, and because there is no dusk here, and darkness can descend with sudden abruptness, we went first to where the diggers were working.

The river flows along the bottom of a deep gorge. Its bed is shallow, sandy, and gravelly. Its every centimetre has been ploughed, and you can see everywhere deep craters, pits, holes, ravines. Over this battlefield swarm crowds of half-naked, black-skinned people, streaming with sweat and water, all of them feverish, in a trance. For there is a peculiar climate here, one of excitement, desire, greed, risk, an atmosphere not unlike that of a darkly lit casino. It's as though an invisible roulette wheel were spinning somewhere near, capriciously whirling. But the dominant noises here are the hollow tapping of hoes digging through the gravel, the rustle of sand shaken through handheld sieves, and the monotonous utterances, neither calls nor songs, made by the men working at the bottom of the gorge. It doesn't look as if these diggers are finding anything much, putting much aside. They shake the troughs, pour water into them, strain them, inspect the sand in the palm of their hand, hold it up to the light, throw everything back into the river.

And yet sometimes they do find something. If you gaze up to the top of the gorge, to the slopes of the hills that it intersects, you will see, in the shade of mango trees, under the thin umbrellas of acacias and tattered palms, the tents of Arabs. They are gold merchants from the Sahara, from neighbouring Niger, from

Nidjamena and from Nubia. Dressed in white djellabas and snowy, gorgeously wound turbans, they sit idly in tent entrances drinking tea and smoking ornate water pipes. From time to time, one of the exhausted, sinewy black diggers climbs up to them from the bottom of the crowded gorge. He squats in front of an Arab, takes out and unrolls a piece of paper. In its crease lie several grains of gold sand. The Arab looks at them indifferently, deliberates, calculates, then names a figure. The grime-covered black Cameroonian, master of this land and of this river—it is, after all, his country and his gold—cannot contest the price, or argue for a higher one. Another Arab would give him the same measly sum. And the next one, too. There is only one price. This is a monopoly.

Darkness descends, the gorge empties and grows quiet, and one can no longer see its interior, now a black, undifferentiated chasm. We walk to the settlement, called Colomine. It is a hastily thrown together little town, so makeshift and scruffy that its inhabitants will have no qualms abandoning it once the gold in the river runs out. Shack leaning against shack, hovel against hovel, the streets of slums all emptying into the main one, which has bars and shops and where evening and nightlife take place. There is no electricity. Oil lamps, torches, fires and candles are burning everywhere. What their glow picks out from the darkness is flickering and wobbly. Here, some silhouettes slip by; over there, someone's face suddenly appears, an eye glitters, a hand emerges. That piece of tin, that's a roof. That flash you just saw, that's a knife. And that piece of plank—who knows what it's from and what purpose it serves. Nothing connects, arranges itself, can be composed into a whole. We know only that this darkness all around us is in motion, that it has shapes and emits sounds; that with the assistance of light we can bring bits of it up to the surface and momentarily observe them, but that as soon as the light goes out, everything will escape us and vanish. I saw hundreds of faces in Colomine, heard dozens of conversations, passed countless people walking, bustling about, sitting. But because of the way the images shimmered in the flickering flames of the lamps, because of their augmentation and the speed with which they followed one another, I am unable to connect a single face with a distinct individual or a single voice with some particular person that I met there.

In the morning we drove south, to the great forest. First, however, was the Kadeï river, which runs through the jungle (it is a tributary of the Sangha river, which flows into the Congo river at Yumbi and Bolobo). In keeping with the operative local principle that a thing broken will never be repaired, our ferry looked like something fit only for the scrap heap. But the three little boys scampering around it knew exactly how to compel the monster into motion. The ferry: a huge, rectangular, flat metal box. Above it, a metal wire stretching across the river. Turning a squeaky crank, alternately tightening and releasing the wire, the boys move the ferry (with us and the car on board)—slowly, ever so slowly—from one bank to the other. Of course, this operation can succeed only when the current is sluggish and somnolent. Were it to twitch, to come alive, suddenly we would end up, carried off by the Kadeï, the Sangha and the Congo, somewhere in the Atlantic.

After that—driving, plunging into the forest—sinking, slipping, into the labyrinths, tunnels and underworlds of some alien, green, dusky, impenetrable realm. One cannot compare the tropical forest with any European forest or with any equatorial jungle. Europe's forests are beautiful and rich, but they are of average scale and their trees are of moderate height: we can imagine ourselves climbing to the top of even the highest ash or oak. And the jungle is a vortex, a giant knot of tangled branches, roots, shrubs and vines, a heated and compressed nature endlessly proliferating, a green cosmos.

This forest is different. It is monumental, its trees—thirty, fifty, and more metres high—are gigantic, perfectly straight, loosely positioned, maintaining clearly delineated distances between one another and growing out of the ground with virtually no undercover. Driving into the forest, in between these sky-high sequoias, mahogany trees, and others I do not recognize, I have the sensation of stepping across the threshold of a great cathedral, squeezing into the interior of an Egyptian pyramid, or standing suddenly amid the skyscrapers of Fifth Avenue.

The journey here is often a torment. There are stretches of road so pitted and rough that for all intents and purposes one cannot drive, and the car is flung about like a boat on a stormy sea. The only vehicles that can deal with these surfaces are the gigantic machines with engines like the underbellies of steam locomotives, which the French, Italians, Greeks and Dutch use to export timber from here to Europe. For the forest is being cut down day and night, its surface shrinking, its trees disappearing. You constantly come across large, empty clearings, with huge fresh stumps sticking out of the earth. The screech of saws, their whistling, penetrating echo, carries for kilometres.

Somewhere in this forest, in which we all appear so small, live others smaller still—its permanent inhabitants. It is rare to see them. We pass their straw huts along the way. But there is no one around. The owners are somewhere deep in the forest. They are hunting birds, gathering berries, chasing lizards, searching for honey. In front of each house, hanging on a stick or stretched out on a line, are owl's feathers, the claws of an anteater, the corpse of a scorpion, or the tooth of a snake. The message is in the manner in which these trifles are arranged: they probably tell of the owners' whereabouts.

At nightfall we spotted a simple country church and beside it a humble house, the rectory. We had arrived at our destination. Somewhere, in one of the rooms, an oil lamp was burning, and a small, wavering glow fell through the open door on to the porch. We entered. It was dark and quiet inside. After a moment, a tall, thin man in a light habit came out to greet us: Father Jan, from southern Poland. He had an emaciated, sweaty face with large, blazing eyes. He had malaria, was clearly running a fever, his body probably wracked by chills and cramps. Suffering, weak and listless, he spoke in a quiet voice. He wanted to play the host somehow, to offer us something, but from his embarrassed gestures and aimless puttering about it was plain he didn't have the means, and didn't know how. An old woman arrived from the village and began to warm up some rice for us. We drank water, then a boy brought a bottle of banana beer. 'Why do you stay here, father?' I asked. 'Why don't you leave?' He gave the impression of a man in whom some small part had already died. There was already something missing. 'I cannot,' he answered. 'Someone has to guard the church.' And he gestured with his hand towards the black shape visible through the window.

I went to lie down in the adjoining room. I couldn't sleep. Suddenly, the words of an old altar boy's response started to play in my head: *Pater noster, qui es in caeli...Fiat voluntas tua...sed libera nos a malo...*

In the morning, the boy whom I had seen the previous evening beat with a hammer on a dented metal wheel rim hanging on a wire. This served as the bell. Stanislaw and Jan were celebrating morning mass in the church, a mass in which the boy and I were the sole participants. □

THE LOST CITY
Isabel Hilton

BEIJING NOTEBOOK
OCTOBER 2000

The first major biography of an anti-colonial icon: a thoughtful,
critical and moving account of Fanon's life and violent times.

'This year's
biographical tour
de force'
Richard Gott,
New Statesman

FRANTZ FANON

A LIFE I DAVID MACEY

£25 Hardback

Decca Aitkenhead visited Thailand during a world tour of dance clubs. *Strange Ways*, her account of this journey, will be published by Fourth Estate later this year. She has written for the London *Independent* and the *Guardian*.

Manuel Bauer is a founder member of Lookat, the Swiss photographers' agency. His interest in Tibet and Tibetans in exile dates back to 1990.

James Campbell's biography of James Baldwin, *Talking at the Gates*, will be reissued by University of California Press later this year. His books include *This Is the Beat Generation* (Vintage/University of California Press) and *Paris Interzone* which will be reissued this year by Vintage in the UK.

Isabel Hilton studied in China between 1973 and 1975. She is the author of *The Search for the Panchen Lama* (Penguin/W. W. Norton). She is a columnist for the *Guardian* and is writing a book about Cuba to be published next year (Viking/W. W. Norton).

Ian Jack is the editor of *Granta*. The sources for his piece 'The 12.10 to Leeds' include *All Change: British Railway Privatization* edited by Freeman and Shaw (McGraw Hill), and the library of the Institution of Civil Engineering.

Ryszard Kapuscinski's 'The Lazy River' is taken from *The Shadow of the Sun* to be published in June (Penguin/Knopf). In the 1960s and 70s he was the Polish Press Agency's only foreign correspondent. His books include *The Soccer War* and *Imperium* (Granta Books/Vintage).

Sunil Khilnani teaches at the University of London. He is the author of *The Idea of India*, published by Penguin in the UK and Farrar, Straus & Giroux in the US. He is writing a biography of Jawaharlal Nehru.

Ian McEwan's 'Dunkirk' is taken from a novel-in-progress to be published by Jonathan Cape in 2002. His most recent novel, *Amsterdam* (Vintage/Anchor), won the Booker Prize in 1998.

John Ryle is a regional specialist working for aid agencies and human rights organizations in Africa and the Middle East.

Dayanita Singh's photographs are part of her exhibition, *I Am What I Am*, at the Ikon Gallery, Birmingham until May 13, 2001. They will also be included in a book of her photographs to be published by Scalo in autumn this year. She is a member of Network Photographers. She lives in Delhi.

Simon Winchester's book about the birth of contemporary geology, *The Map that Changed the World*, will be published later this year by Penguin in the UK. He is currently working on a study of the explosion of Krakatoa in 1883.

Teun Voeten, whose photo essay on Sierra Leone appeared in *Granta* 72, is represented by Panos pictures.